Native American Religions

An Introduction

Second Edition

Native American Religions

An Introduction

Second Edition

SAM D. GILL

The University of Colorado at Boulder

Australia • Brazil • Japan • Korea • Mexico • Singapore • Spain • United Kingdom • United States

WADSWORTH
CENGAGE Learning™

**Native American Religions:
An Introduction, Second Edition**
Sam D. Gill

Publisher: Holly J. Allen

Religion Editor: Steve Wainwright

Assistant Editors: Lee McCracken,
Anna Lustig

Editorial Assistant:
Barbara Hillaker

Marketing Manager:
Worth Hawes

Marketing Assistant:
Andrew Keay

Advertising Project Manager:
Vicky Wan

Executive Art Director:
Maria Epes

Print/Media Buyer:
Emma Claydon

Composition Buyer:
Ben Schroeter

Permissions Editor:
Audrey Pettengill

Production Service: Shepherd, Inc.

Copy Editor: Amy Freitag

Cover Designer: Yvo Riezebos

Cover Image: Punchstock Images

Compositor: Shepherd, Inc.

For product information and
technology assistance, contact us at **Cengage Learning
Customer & Sales Support, 1-800-354-9706**

For permission to use material from this text or product,
submit all requests online at **www.cengage.com/permissions**
Further permissions questions can be e-mailed to
permissionrequest@cengage.com

ISBN-13: 978-0-534-62600-6

ISBN-10: 0-534-62600-9

Wadsworth Cengage Learning
20 Davis Drive
Belmont, CA 94002-3098
USA

Cengage Learning is a leading provider of customized learning
solutions with office locations around the globe, including
Singapore, the United Kingdom, Australia, Mexico, Brazil, and
Japan. Locate your local office at **www.cengage.com/global**

Cengage Learning products are represented in Canada by
Nelson Education, Ltd.

To learn more about Wadsworth, visit
www.cengage.com/wadsworth

Purchase any of our products at your local college store or at our
preferred online store **www.cengagebrain.com**

Printed in Canada
2 3 4 5 14 13 12 11

For Jennifer Robin and Fatumata

Contents

Preface

Native American cultures are familiar to most Americans, being widely treated in literature, art, and film. Native Americans are inseparable from the American identity—its people, landscapes, arts, and history—and it is commonly recognized that rituals, ceremonials, and mythological stories are an important part of Native American cultures.

Few Americans would disagree that the history of the European-American encounter with Native Americans is a national dishonor and that to avoid further error on this path we must completely reshape the terms of the relationship. The basic terms must include less presumption about and more sensitivity to the worldviews and religious values of the Native American people themselves. President John F. Kennedy spoke precisely to this point when he said, "It seems a basic requirement to study the history of our Indian people. America has much to learn about the heritage of our American Indians. Only through this study can we as a nation do what must be done if our treatment of the American Indians is not to be marked down for all time as a national disgrace."[1]

Perhaps with the importance of this heritage in mind, and recognizing that religion is so essential to it, the U.S. Congress passed a bill, signed into law in 1978, establishing as the policy of the United States "to protect and preserve for American Indians their inherent right of freedom to believe, express, and exercise the traditional religions . . . including but not limited to access to sites, use and possession of sacred objects, and the freedom to worship through ceremonials and traditional rites" (Public Law 95-341). The law has had far too little effect.

The importance of the Native American heritage is reflected in the great ethnographic effort begun in the nineteenth century that produced an unprecedented record of Native American cultures. A large portion of this record documents the religious aspects of culture.

As a student of religion, I have been perplexed that, with widespread public interest, with unprecedented resources including enormous amounts among living Native Americans, with the inseparability of Native American cultures from the very identity of America, with presidential proclamations and federal laws, systematic attention to Native American religions has yet to find a substantial place in the academic study of religion.

The fields of anthropology, linguistics, and folklore, among others, have developed and matured with a large number of scholars devoted to studying various aspects of Native American cultures. While there is no counterpart in religious studies, students of religion have benefited from the theoretical developments in these other fields of study. Religion is clearly a dimension of Americanist studies, but it remains undeveloped.

In writing and revising this book, my foremost goal has been to provide an introduction to Native American religions, focusing on the cultures of North America. The aim is not so much to introduce data and facts as to introduce an academically and humanistically useful way of trying to appreciate and understand the complexity and diversity of Native American religions. I have also examined aspects of European-American history in a search for the sources of widespread misunderstandings about the character of Native American religions.

Many of the issues I discuss have been actualized through my own experiences and I present them as such. The many interpretations I suggest are also based on premises that I have accepted. This is not to suggest, however, that my interpretations or approaches are the only valid ones.

In preparation for revising this book, I was a bit dismayed at pervasive careless and vague use of language, yet I was surprised to find that many of the things I am presently thinking and writing about, things I thought were pretty new to me, were actually present in this book, though undeveloped.

I extensively revised the text though leaving the order and principal examples pretty much as they were. The concepts and approaches are expanded and tightened; the language extensively revised. I replaced a concluding chapter with a new Epilogue "Stories." My book *Storytracking: Texts, Stories, and Histories in Central Australia* (Oxford University Press, 1998) and the writing I am currently doing on play and dancing center on the creative and positive aspects of the playful ambiguity of story. As brief as it is, this epilogue is an offering to open new discourse in the academic study of Native American religions as well as a small exploration into a different academic style.

The suggestions of a number of generous and diligent colleagues have been invaluable to my revision and their encouragement was important to my doing the work at all. I particularly want to thank Fritz Detwiler, Adrian College; Greg Johnson, Franklin and Marshall College; Russell Kirkland, University of

Georgia; Pamela Jean Owens, University of Nebraska at Omaha; and Kenneth Morrison, Arizona State University.

Now I return to completing my books *To Risk Meaning Nothing: Essays on Play* and *Dancing*. I continue my interest in dancing both through my teaching, research, and writing of dance and music related courses at the University of Colorado and beyond that as a teacher and dancer of salsa and other Latin American dances.

One way we keep track of ourselves is the development of our children. I dedicated the first edition of this book to my daughter, Jennifer Robin, then seven years old. Now Jenny is 28. She has a degree in ethnomusicology, is married to a musician and griot from Senegal, has a beautiful daughter named Fatumata, and is co-owner and partner with me in our business Bantaba World Dance and Music, now in its sixth year. I'm excited about the kinds of stories that my granddaughter will be making as an American African exposed to many cultures, dances, languages, and musics. Certainly the hope of our future is with her.

NOTES

1. John F. Kennedy, introduction to Alvin M. Josephy, ed., *The American Heritage Book of Indians* (New York: American Heritage, 1961), p. 7.

1

❦

Maps and Territories

Beginning this introduction to Native American religions, it is essential to place both the subject matter and the academic approach in the appropriate context: the history of contact that has played a major role in the understanding and shaping of Native Americans and their religions for more than half a millennium. To ignore this historical background would be to pretend that the subject matter can be understood both more clearly and on different terms than is possible. To ignore the effects of the involvement by non–Native Americans on both the cultures studied and the approach taken to study them is not only misleading it also deters.

Rather than beginning with the earliest archaeological evidence of Native American religions and developing the study from that origin, the beginning must be even earlier, not in a temporal but in a logical sense, by considering the ideas and images that have shaped our perceptions and conceptions of Native Americans and their religions—ideas and images fostered by the earliest stages of European contact. This approach clarifies why, in the study of Native Americans, it has seemed so important for us to locate Native American origins geographically and temporally, whereas Native Americans seem generally uninterested in these findings, and why aspects of their lives and cultures are classified as religious, when they often do not seem to make such a distinction.

ORBIS TERRARUM:
THE ISLAND OF THE EARTH

In 1492 Columbus sailed westward on the premise that he would reach the east coast of Asia. In Europe at that time, it was believed that the world was composed of the three continents Europe, Asia, and Africa—all joined to form a large *Orbis Terrarum,* or island of the earth. This island, though positioned on a sphere, was surrounded by the seas, which confined the land and gave it boundaries, limitations, and definition. The seas were associated with death, chaos, and mystery, for they stood beyond the defined earth. Furthermore, the Christian beliefs prevailing at that time in Europe held that God had created one world and that all people in that world were descendants of Adam and Eve.

It is in the context of this cosmology, this view of the structure of the universe, that Christopher Columbus reacted when he sighted the land he believed to be the east coast of Asia. Given his understanding of the earth it could have been nothing else. He knew what the lands and people were supposed to be like from the accounts of Marco Polo and others who, traveling east overland, had been there. Although his observations did not correspond to their accounts, in his own mind he had accomplished what he had set out to do. Each of his three subsequent voyages was made to further confirm the correspondence of what he found with what he expected. Each time, however, the facts he collected presented more evidence that proved inconsistent with his expectations. Yet even after four voyages and considerable consternation at these discrepancies, Columbus remained solidly of one mind.

Look more closely at two observational aspects of these early voyages—the lands and the peoples—in order to clarify what was taking place.

On Columbus's third voyage in 1498, he had decided to sail farther south than he had before in order to find the lower end of the Golden Chersonese (Malay Peninsula)—which would, he believed, reveal the passage to the Indian Ocean. He landed in a gulf in what is presently Venezuela. He wanted to consider this an island near the passage to the Indian Ocean, but the water in the gulf was fresh, not salty. He was forced to recognize that he had landed not on a small island, but on a land mass of continental magnitude. This raised for him a major problem, because Marco Polo and others who had journeyed to Asia through the Indian Ocean had reported that nothing but open sea lay to the south of the Golden Chersonese. Columbus found himself having to explain not only to others, but to himself, the existence of this great land mass he had found. This was more difficult because of the religious belief in one God-created world. To suggest that another world existed would be heresy, a declaration of the existence of some world not of God's creation. His dilemma was resolved only by suggesting that this land was the lost paradise wherein lay the Garden of Eden, which the ancients had reported to be "at the end of the East." This decision permitted him to hold to his belief that the lands to the north that he had charted—that is, the southern coasts of the islands now known as Haiti/Santo Domingo and Cuba—were part of the mainland of Asia.

The voyage of Amerigo Vespucci (1501–1502) charted much of the east coast of South America and confirmed the great size of this "new world." He too was unable to give it identity because of the cosmological expectations of his time. Though both Columbus and Vespucci referred to it as a new world, they meant the world referred to by the ancients, and thus a world created by God.

Not until 1507 did the data collected from these voyages produce a shift in the very conception of the shape and nature of the world. The resolution to the situation was first stated in the *Cosmographiae Introductio* published by the Academy of St. Dié. It maintained that the world was still one but that a fourth part had been found. It differed from the other parts in its characteristic features. They were continents, but this fourth part was an island surrounded by the sea. The extensive use of Vespucci's information apparently led to naming the island America, the feminine form of Amerigo, corresponding with the feminine names Europe and Asia.

Edmundo O'Gorman has shown that these facts amount to quite a different understanding of events than historians have usually described. Instead of attributing to Columbus the discovery of America, a position that O'Gorman shows is finally impossible to reconcile with what is known, he argues that America was not *discovered* at all. It was *invented!* In light of the late fifteenth-century beliefs, there was no basis for speculating even the possible existence of a continent separate from *Orbis Terrarum*. To have thought so, let alone to proclaim its discovery, was not even a possibility to the minds of Columbus and Vespucci. The land about which these and other explorers gathered data had no acceptable identity or reality to Europeans apart from its designation as the east coast of Asia until the gathered facts led to the invention of the idea of a fourth part of the world. This invention was the result of the constructive extension and transformation of the cosmology believed at the time—and it was a religious invention at that. The notion of invention is necessary simply because one cannot discover what one cannot even imagine as a possibility.[1]

Columbus called the peoples he saw *los Indios,* in English "the Indians," a term apparently used at the time to refer to all people east of the Indus River. To make such a designation simply placed or identified these people as among the known descendants of Adam and Eve. To have identified them otherwise would have been impossible, for it was believed that all human beings descended from God's initial creation. In the most general sense, Columbus had little choice. The only other possibility was not to see them as people at all, an alternative some people accepted in the early sixteenth century. At another level, it was a we/they designation: we are Europeans, and they are Indians, a people of east Asia.

But the invention of America, the designation of a fourth part of the world, did not resolve the problem of identifying the people on this fourth part. While they had to be descendants of Adam and Eve and their designation as *los Indios* held, for they lived east of the Indus River, the remaining problem was how they had come to occupy the lands of America. By 1535, the Spanish historian Gonzalo Fernandez de Oviedo had already postulated the existence of a narrow sea passage, the forerunner of our present theory of migration across the Bering Strait.[2]

It is curious that the theories of the origin of Native Americans always conclude with the point of contact in Asia—or, though less often accepted, in Europe or Africa. Why does the academic study of Native Americans trace them backward in time and space only to their point of departure from the Old World and stop there? Perhaps it is because there is a religious motivation behind this, rooted in the late fifteenth- and early sixteenth-century beliefs in the unity of humankind. Although their premises are now stated in humanistic terms, archaeologists and anthropologists have been persistently working on the old theological problem created by *los Indios,* and the best solution has been, and still is, in the establishment of a kinship connection between Native American people and any people of the other three parts of the world.

Given this historical background, the term Indian is not a white invention, as Robert Berkhofer has called it,[3] but the application of common terminology used in the early sixteenth-century Christian world to designate people of the Far East. From that perspective, the term is wholly accurate in its application to Native Americans. The application of the term Indian to the native people of America is similar to Columbus's belief that he had found the western route to Asia. Through four voyages he saw only what the terms of his expectations and worldview permitted him to see. The present-day use of the term Indian, and even the alternatives Native American or even indigenous, is not so different. It is a product of encounter and is fully shaped by European expectations about the world and its people.

Thus, the study of Native American religions, on the basis argued here, is actually more a study of European views of the people living in the lands labeled America on the map of Europeans.

This study is a mapping of human cultures analogous to the mapping of the physical territory. Yet, there is no satellite imaging that would give us a sense of a God's eye or objective view. All maps are the invention of encounter and expectation.

ALL MANKIND IS ONE

In mid-August 1550, the Council of the Fourteen met in Valladolid at the summons of Charles V of Spain to hear arguments presented by two men on matters dealing with the conquest of the New World and to decide on the issues debated.[4] On the first day, the Renaissance scholar Juan Gines de Sepúlveda gave a three-hour presentation of his case. The next day his opponent, a Dominican who had spent some forty-five years in the New World, Bartolome de Las Casas, began presenting his position. He continued for five days, reading only select parts of extensive treatises he had prepared. The issue to be decided was how to Christianize the Indians. The arguments hinged on what manner of beings were these people so that their capacity for receiving Christianity and European civilization might be determined. Sepúlveda's position was based on the histories of the New World, primarily those written by Gonzalo Fernandez de Oviedo, which portrayed a negative image of these people. Sepúlveda linked this image with Aristotle's definition of natural slavery in order to argue that the Indians were slaves by nature. This position advocated the system of *encomiendaro,* which permitted colonists to use the natives for their own profit as well as to use acts of war and violence to conquer the people so that they might be Christianized.

Las Casas refuted Sepúlveda's arguments based on his half-century of experience living among people of the New World. He showed they were a noble people developed in the arts, in language, and in government; that they were gentle and eager to learn; and that they were even quick to accept Christianity. Though the council debated the issue it supported Sepúlveda.

Leading up to this famous event is a history of debate over the nature of the Indians that began before America was invented, commencing with the beginning of colonization in the late fifteenth century. During the first half of the sixteenth century, the issue had been much discussed and the debate had split into two camps. One side viewed Indians negatively as brutes, animals, evil, whereas the other saw them as perhaps savage, yet noble.

This early debate illustrates the nature of the dynamics involved from 1500 to the present in formulating the dominating images of Native Americans. Recasting the opposing views of Sepúlveda and Las Casas into the terms of a we/they relationship provides clarification.[5] Sepúlveda saw his own culture as Christian, civilized, learned, and advanced in the arts and production of material goods; the Indians were a perfect counterimage: pagan, uncivilized, incapable of learning, unable to govern themselves, beastly, inhumane, and barbarian. In short, the Indians were, by their nature, only fit to be slaves to Europeans. Las Casas, citing scripture, took a stance on the basis of his religious convictions and maintained that all humankind is one by the fact of God's single creation. "He hath made of one blood all nations of men for to dwell on all the face of the earth."[6] Further, he recognized the high status of the Indians' nobility and went to great lengths to demonstrate their likeness to Europeans in humanity, civility, ability to learn, and artistry. Hence for Las Casas the only difference was that Europeans were Christian and the Indians were not. It became his lifework to bring Christianity to them, thus resolving any distinction at all. He also insisted that Christianity be brought to them without violence, enslavement, or mistreatment.

It is not only significant that these two men came to represent two sides of an issue debated through much of the sixteenth century but also, to an extent, they still represent the major positions from which images of Native Americans are created. And even as Sepúlveda won the debate over Las Casas, the successors to his position have tended to be the more dominant throughout the last four and a half centuries.

Even though the earliest explorers, colonists, and historians noted differences between the native tribes in terms of their physical structure, food habits, skin color, and friendliness, the image of the Indian had a unitary character. Even as it became known that many different tribes, languages, and ways of life existed, Native Americans continued to be labeled under the single concept of Indians. This sense of unity is maintained by referring to tribal or cultural designations as a species variety of the genus Indian. Even after Las

Casas's fifty years of contact, the variety of his data gave way to the creation of a singular image of the Indian as a noble savage.

There are two relatively clear reasons for the steadfast insistence on subjugating the observed variety of people and types to a simplified stereotypical image. The first concerns the nature of we/they relationships. The relationship itself requires that we identify the characteristics that distinguish us from them. Owing to the developments in communication resulting from the invention of the printing press in the fifteenth century and from more extensive travel, the sense of a general European identity was growing. The colonization of America was also helpful in making the character of the European distinct by the foil provided in the image of the Indian. Simply stated, many Europeans followed the argument of Sepúlveda by seeing what they needed to see in the New World, a simple image by its contrast and opposition to the defining of themselves.

The second factor involved in this unity of image is the failure to distinguish between biological and cultural classifications. Cultures were designated by a defining image, as biological species were defined by a set of distinctive features. This is just as clear in identifying an image of the European as in creating an image of the Indian. The confusing and blending together of national character, race, and culture led to the stereotypical images of nations and continents that remained unchallenged until the twentieth century, and we continue to live with this heritage.[7]

Historically, there have been many unfortunate consequences of cultures and peoples understanding and relating with one another in terms of simplified constructed and ungrounded stereotypes. Native Americans have often been ignored or treated as children by the majority of America. On the other hand, particularly after Native Americans were physically suppressed, they have been viewed as admirable in contrast to a disenchanting view of European-American values and ways of life. One of the most far-reaching results of the image of Native Americans is created by contrasting that image with the espoused European admiration of history, of embracing and engineering change in the form of progress. The counterimage thus thrust on Native Americans is that of a people who are timeless and ahistorical, changeless and nonprogressive. Native Americans are strongly encouraged to act according to this image, even though it violates all observed facts. The judgement of how real a Native American is has often been based on how closely he or she comes to the constructed image, which projects back to precontact times. This image shapes expectations about dress, about places of residence, about language, about social activities, about nearly every aspect of life. The Native American group or individual who does not measure up to these images is somehow, in this view, not really Indian.

Similarly, the image of Native Americans serves as a counterimage for civilization, they have not been permitted to enter civilization without, of course, changing their identities. The relationships of government and religious institutions to Native Americans have been greatly shaped by images, for these relationships have been based on an assumption that they are culturally deprived and that those who approach them must do so as guardians and philanthropists.[8]

Finally, and most importantly to the present concern, the counterimage created for Indians depicts them as pagan or heathen, usually construed as meaning they are without religion. In describing the first Native Americans Columbus briefly encountered, he wrote that "they do not hold any creed nor are they idolators";[9] and Vespucci wrote, "They have no church, no religion and are not idolators."[10] Even though the facts are overwhelmingly in contrast to the view that Native Americans have no religions, such an image obscures these facts. According to this image, Native Americans are not supposed to have religions, at least in any terms comparable to Western religions. It is noteworthy that until very recently, American religious historians have totally avoided even mentioning Native American religions and have included them in American religion only in relationship to Christian missionization.[11]

While an understanding of Native Americans is not possible without some preconceived images of them, critically examining these images and acknowledging their influence provides an important beginning. On one hand there is no choice but to hold to the conviction of Las Casas, although on humanistic rather than Christian theological grounds, that all humankind is one; otherwise the subject would be merely an interest in peculiarities and oddities. On the other hand, however, the notion of a stereotypical image argued by both Sepúlveda and Las Casas and the simple, unified identity of Native Americans must be rejected. Although all human beings have certain capacities and characteristics in common, the expression of these may vary greatly. It is important to be sensitive to that variety among Native Americans, both in the diversity of the many peoples and cultures, and in the diversity of individuals within every group. Attention to differences, and what such differences reveal and suggest, is far more important than the effort to reduce all differences to unity.

HOMO RELIGIOSUS

Introducing the term religion as an aspect of Native American life presents many difficulties. The term's origins lie in Western, not Native American, history, and the academic study of religion remains largely of interest only to Western religious and academic institutions. Only in the last century or so has religion been generally accepted as a study relevant to the nature of humankind. And only in the last several decades has the distinction between teaching the doctrines of religion and teaching about religion as an aspect of humanity been partially clarified and accepted so that it can be legally taught in state-supported colleges and universities. This acceptance signals that the Western intellectual understanding of the term religion is undergoing considerable, even radical, change. Thus, it is difficult, if not also tedious, to define the term that names our principal category of study.

It is difficult to find words in Native American languages that adequately approximate religion. This means, at the least, that an academically articulated understanding of religion is not linguistically distinguished in the same way by Native Americans. Furthermore, since the word religion has often been used in a narrow way by ethnographers, missionaries, and government agencies from the time of Columbus, many Native Americans have often abhorred the use of the word. They associate it with the grossest of European misunderstandings of their cultures and with flagrant violations of their privacy and way of life.

Columbus considered religion to be equal to "creed and church," as did Vespucci. They equated religion and Christianity, and while they probably did not expect to find Christianity among Indians, they appeared to expect some corruption of religion in the form of idolatry. Yet they reported finding not even that. For them, Native Americans had nothing that resembled religion. How the term religion is understood determines what is recognized in Native American cultures as religious. The generally accepted proposition that underlies the study of religion as a general human phenomenon is that religion is a characteristic distinctive of being human. From one point of view, that is, the premise that underlies the academic study of religion is that among the many ways of distinguishing being human is that humans are religious. It follows that Native Americans, as all humans, are religious.

As a guiding statement, the religious includes those images, actions, and symbols that both express and define the extent and character of the world, especially those that provide the cosmic framework in which human life finds meaning and the terms of its fulfillment. The religious also includes those actions, processes, and symbols through which life is lived in order that it may be meaningful and purposive. But while this understanding refers to the grandest level of human action, conception, and imagination, for Native Americans aspects of religion occur in stories of creation, heroes, tricksters, and fools; in architecture, art, and orientations in the landscape; in ritual drama, costumes, masks, and ceremonial paraphernalia; and in relation to hunting, farming, and fishing. Grand cosmological schemes and religious ideas are found in the rudest, most common materials and circumstances as well as in highly developed poetic, intellectual, and artistic forms.

This understanding of religion focuses on meaning, but clarification is needed. Language and the study of language commonly serves as the model for understanding meaning. With language as the model, meaning is understood as the articulable, the translatable, and often considered to be singular. Of a religious situation, thus the question is "what does it mean?" The emphasis here is more on the meaningful than on specifiable meanings. The meaningful is not reduceable to a simple statement of meaning. The meaningful is that reservoir from which meaning is even possible. To understand something as full of meaning is often simply the awareness of its ineffability and vastness, its opacity, rather than its specifiability and articulability, its clarity. In the study of Native American religions, as with all religions, it is important to adumbrate the fullness, the potentiality, the richness for meaning, as expansive enterprise, rather than to reduce the religious to a simple statement of explanation.

The presentation of Native American religions usually entails organizing the massive quantities of data either by geographic area or type of phenomena. Although the data are essential to the understanding of Native American religions, the primary task of an introductory study is not the presentation of facts. The facts are meaningful in terms of the questions asked of them. Thus, this study must be organized directly around specific questions. Abundant culturally specific data will be presented in the process of considering these questions. The primary intention is neither a complete or orderly presentation of facts.

We are, at this point, still in the boat with Columbus. We may believe that we are finding some of the answers to our questions. Perhaps the advice that can best hold a rein on our errors is to remember that the task is charting maps of the territory we circumscribe by the term "Native American religions" and to recall, as Jonathan Z. Smith has so aptly phrased it, that "map is not territory."[12] This is an introductory mapping from non–Native American perspectives of the imagined territory, Native American religions.

NOTES

1. The information on this story of Columbus is presented in Edmundo O'Gorman, *The Invention of America: An Inquiry into the Historical Nature of the New World and the Meaning of Its History* (Bloomington: Indiana University Press, 1961), especially pp. 71–125.

2. Ibid., p. 138.

3. Robert F. Berkhofer, Jr., *The White Man's Indian: Images of the American Indian from Columbus to the Present* (New York: Knopf, 1978), p. 3.

4. The heading as well as much of the material presented in this section is drawn from Lewis Hanke, *All Mankind Is One: A Study of the Disputation between Bartolome de Las Casas and Juan Gines de Sepúlveda in 1550 on the Intellectual and Religious Capacity of the American Indians* (DeKalb: Northern Illinois University Press, 1974).

5. For a discussion of how the we/they relationship is fundamental to the nature of comparison—and how it has been reflected in various attitudes and scholarly styles in the history of the comparative study of cultures—see Jonathan Z. Smith, *"Adde Parvum Parvo Magnus Acervus Erit,"* History of Religions 11 (1971): 67–90.

6. Hanke, *All Mankind Is One*, p. 57, quoting the use of Acts 17:26 by Las Casas.

7. Berkhofer, *The White Man's Indian*, pp. 23–25.

8. Ibid., p. 26.

9. Ibid., p. 6.

10. Ibid., p. 8.

11. An exception to this general avoidance is the book by Catherine Albanese, *America: Religions and Religion* (Belmont, Ca: Wadsworth, 1981) that devotes a chapter to Native American religions.

12. Jonathan Z. Smith, *Map Is Not Territory* (Leiden: E. J. Brill, 1979), especially the essay "Map Is Not Territory," pp. 289–310.

2

〰

The Place to Begin

There are a large number of Native American cultures in North America. Each culture is distinct, with its own language, its own history, its own religious institutions, traditions, practices, and beliefs. This diversity and complexity make it difficult to find a starting point for considering Native American religions. Choosing the terminology and categories of any one tradition or those of Western religious traditions as representative prejudices all the consideration of the others. The bias of point of view is unavoidable, yet it is important to be mindful of limitations, potential prejudice, and error. One way in which many traditions map the territories of their own world is with stories of creation. These stories map the world, its values, categories, principles, and relationships. If religion is expressed and practiced through these most basic and defining elements, then the examination of creation stories will reveal important aspects of religion. It is common to refer to such stories as mythology or, more exactly, as creation or cosmogonic mythology. The distinctive marker of these stories, being set "in the beginning," is not a historical reckoning. It is rather a way to designate events as beyond question and doubt, beyond precedent. Nor does mythology mean false or scientifically false, yet believed by the primitive or unsophisticated. A paper map of a geographical area uses symbols and conventions to indicate ways in which the gross or raw territory can be understood as significant, for example, rainfall, elevation, fuel service stations, cities, populations, temperatures, and so on. Stories of creation or origination can be understood as an important way people of a culture both learn and transmit what is most fundamentally valued.

An extension of this map analogy is that creation stories set the boundaries and terms for many of the other maps held by a given culture. Therefore, creation stories are legends in more than one sense.

The consideration of several examples will show the diversity of ways in which religious principles, beliefs, and practices are mapped by stories of creation.

RELIGION AND THE SHAPE OF THE WORLD

Zuni: The Middle Place

In 1528, the Spaniard Cabeza de Vaca survived a shipwreck near the American shores and wandered over what is now northern Mexico and parts of Texas until 1536, when he was rescued. He recounted stories told to him by Indians about the existence of seven golden cities at a place called Cibola. When this news reached Spain, an expedition was immediately commissioned to seek these golden cities. It was led by Fray Marcos de Niza, who took with him Estéban, the black slave of Cabeza de Vaca. In May of 1539, this expedition succeeded in forcefully claiming one of seven Zuni villages, Hawikuh, for the King of Spain, but in the conquest Estéban was killed by the Zuni. Marcos de Niza reported seeing from a distance another village. The following year, Spanish explorer Francisco Vasquez de Coronado found and captured the same village and named it Granada. Continuing his conquest of the area, he found a total of seven Zuni villages. The golden color of the sunlit adobe did not impress the Spaniards, and Coronado continued to look for the fabled seven cities of gold. This famed first contact with Native Americans in the territory now known as the United States, occurring more than eighty years before the *Mayflower* sailed, is more than historically important.

While the Spanish did not recognize them as golden cities, to the Zuni the seven villages were not only of a golden hue, but they also embodied meanings fully as precious as was gold to the Spanish.

According to Zuni stories of origin, in the beginning there existed only Awonawilona, an androgynous creator figure, who is conceived as something of a composite of all superhuman beings and is identified with the great vault of the heaven. Awonawilona breathed from his/her heart and created the clouds and waters. With the assistance of other creators, Awonawilona created the universe as it is known to the Zuni. In that first time, "when the earth was soft," the ancestors of the Zuni lived below the earth surface, in dark and crowded caves. The Sun Father created two sons, war gods. Equipped with rainbows and lightning arrows for transportation, these two descended into the fourth world below the earth surface to bring the Zuni people out to the light of the sun. In Zuni, the word for life, *tekohananee*, means daylight and the inner stuff of life, *tse'makwin*, means thoughts and is associated with the head, the heart, and the breath.[1] The Zuni remained near the emergence place where, at intervals of four years, the earth would rumble and other people—the Hopi, the Navajo, the Mexicans—emerged from the lower worlds. They were, according to these stories, the younger brothers and sisters of the Zuni.[2]

The instructions given the Zuni people were to embark upon a journey in search of the "middle place of the world." Searching for many years they traveled in distinct groups, the original Zuni clans and clan affiliations. Each time the Zuni settled, some disaster destroyed their village and forced them to move on, showing them that they had not yet ended their quest for the "middle place." Finally the Zuni met an old man who was a rain priest. Their own rain priest prayed with this man and together they caused so much rain to fall that they knew they had found the "middle place." Any doubts they held were quelled when a water strider came along, spread out its legs, and declared that the middle of the world would be where its heart touched the earth. The location of the Zuni villages were set, one at the place beneath the heart, and one at each place marked by the six feet of the water strider. The esoteric or ceremonial name for the village of Zuni is *Itiwana,* "the middle." Enshrined at the most central spot were the ritual objects of the rain priests marking the exact middle of the world. The Zuni conceive of their world as a large island of earth completely surrounded by oceans. Lakes and springs on the island open to an underground water system that interconnects the oceans.

The seven Zuni villages that Coronado found manifested in the land this Zuni archetype. These villages did not survive the Spanish conquest. The present village of Zuni was founded in 1683 and has remained the only Zuni village except for the temporary camps occupied during agricultural seasons near Zuni farms. It was not until the mid-nineteenth century that ethnographers began to learn that a seven-part cosmological structure existed in the minds of the Zuni people and that this formed the basic division in the village and social organization of the Zuni. The Zuni consider that their village reflects the structure of the cosmos, the basic shape of which is described as an orientation around seven points—the four cardinal directions, the zenith (above), the nadir (below), and the center. Although the present village of Zuni is not neatly layed out with seven distinct physical quarters, shrines and other physical features replicate this fundamental orienting system enacting a correspondence between Zuni and Zuni cosmology.

The sevenfold pattern is a system of orientation within time and space, defined in such a way that each place is distinguished from, yet related to, all other places. The emphasis is as much on interrelationships as on distinctions. The Zuni people are given distinct roles that are complexly interrelated in the terms of place within this sevenfold scheme. Zuni clans are organized into seven groups. Each group, especially those that correspond with the cardinal directions, has distinctions and social roles described in the temporal and spatial terms associated with its place. For example, the Crane, Grouse, and Evergreen-Oak clans are of the north and are associated with winter and with yellow, the color of morning and evening light in the winter as well as the color of the northern auroral lights. The clan symbols are appropriate to the place and its attributes. The crane's flight announces coming winter, the grouse changes its color to white in winter, and the evergreen-oak stays green in winter.

This domain has associations with wind, air, and breath as well as with activities that center on war and destruction. Each cardinal direction has a similar pattern of associations.[3]

For the Zuni life is inseparable from the annual seasonal cycle, the orientation of cosmic directions, and the responsibilities and privileges of the clans. The middle place marks the moment of origination and the place where all other divisions come together. The middle place is one of the seven places distinct from, yet related to, the other six places; but it is also a summation, composite, or symbol of the totality. It is the one point common to all other domains, to all other distinct places. It is the place where all the others interrelate and interact as a totality. This middle place is identified with the heart, the seat of life. Consequently, the middle place is at once the shrine for the most precious ritual objects, the village (whose name means the middle place), and the structure of the cosmos. The creator deity has this same complex character of being both a distinct deity and a composite of all others. In the terms of the Zuni origin and migration stories, the middle place is that place where life is possible, in contrast with those places that are intolerable or where life cannot long exist.

The Zuni notion of *itiwana,* or middle place, corresponds with the organization of the Zuni calendar. The Zuni year is divided into two parts by the solstices, and each part is further divided into six lunar months. The months for each half of the year bear the same names hence both December and June, the months of the solstices, are called *I'kopu,* which means "turning and looking back," referring to the action of the sun reaching its farthermost point and turning back. During each of these winter and summer solstice months, there is a twenty-day period designated as *itiwana.* These middle places in the year are significant times for the celebration and ceremonial marking of a new phase of the year. The making of a new time has the designation of middle place because it denotes the coming together of all the ceremonial societies that, during the remainder of the year, perform separately. It is the temporal grasping of the totality, an act of integration, which gives these twenty-day periods the significance of middle place. The Zuni consider that life itself depends on and proceeds from these middle places in time and space.

Even with this simplified presentation of the Zuni worldview, it is easy to appreciate the rich complexity of the system by which the Zuni place themselves in a way that integrates individual life, clan life, village life, history, and mythology. All human affairs become significant in the terms of their spatial and temporal designations. For the Zuni, the worth of human life is defined by, and evaluated in terms of, orientations in time and space.

For the conquesting Spanish, the worth of a person was measured in the amount of gold possessed; for the Zuni, it was measured in terms of the character of the place on which a person stands.[4]

It seems clear that to attempt to understand anything of Zuni religion, or any other Native American religion, without placing it in the context of this broad framework of the cosmology and religious worldview, would severely limit understanding especially from their perspective. One promising approach to the study of the religions and cultures of other people attempts to discern the shape of reality as the concrete articulation of spatial and temporal distinctions and valuations in story, ritual, and daily life. This approach suggests an important place from which to try mapping worlds and religions in some of the terms of the people involved.

Seneca: The Creator Twins

It is common in many Native American cultures to account for the nature of the world by telling stories of twin brothers whose actions created the world. One brother, the principal creator, attempts to create a perfect world, a utopia for human beings. His brother follows along undoing and reversing much of his brother's work. The current world is the result of the work of both brothers, each a creator in effect. This type of story is known among cultures all over North America. The Seneca version is one example.

> In the beginning before there was an earth, there was a world in the sky. In that place, everything was filled with life that radiated from a giant tree standing in the center of that world. It emitted light half the time and was dark half the time, thus making day and night for the people. Everything there was perfect. There was no want for food. Death did not exist. One family had five sons, and the youngest fell in love with a girl. Feelings of love made this youth weak, for he longed to marry the girl. They were married, but he continued to grow weaker. In a dream, he was told that his brothers should pull up the tree of life by its roots, lest he die. The tree was to provide for the creation of a new world below, and a young tree would grow to replace it in this sky world. The brothers did as instructed, and the tree fell inward into the world below through the hole it had left in the sky. The youth took his wife to the rim of the hole and while they were sitting there, the wind from below blew on the woman and impregnated her. The youth knew that his wife was to be mother to the new world below, so he pushed her off the rim.
>
> Her fall into this new world was eventually broken by a flock of birds that carried her until they could find support for her, since the world was only water. Only the big turtle was strong enough to hold her, and he became the support for the new world. All of the animals dived into the water to seek earth with which to make the world.[5]
>
> When the earth was greatly expanded to its present size, the woman gave birth to a daughter. The daughter approached womanhood, and her mother forbade her to play in the water. But the daughter did so, and the water impregnated her with twins. Even in their mother's womb, the twins began to fight with one another. When it was time for them to be born, one brother was born in the normal way, but the other was too eager and burst a hole in his mother's side, thus killing her. The grandmother buried her daughter, and from her body grew corn and other food plants for the future human beings. She gave the names of *Tarachiawagon,* Good Spirit, and *Tawiskaron,* Bad Spirit, to the boys.

When the twins grew to manhood, they set out on their tasks. The Good Spirit made the form of human beings, male and female, in the dust and breathed life into them. He created the good and useful plants and animals of the world. He created the rivers and lakes. He even made the current run both ways in the streams to make travel easy. Meanwhile, the Bad Spirit busied himself with the creation of annoying and monstrous animals, pests, plant blight, and diseases for human beings. He introduced death. He turned the currents in the streams so they would only run one way. Once he even stole the sun. The Good Spirit tried to reverse these things, but he was not able to reverse them all.

Finally the twin brothers met at the west rim of the world. The Bad Spirit was at this time in the form of a giant. They decided to have a contest to determine which was the stronger and thus settle their struggles once and for all. Their chosen task was the feat of moving the Rocky Mountains. The Bad Spirit tried first and was able to move them, but only a little. When it came time for the Good Spirit to try, he asked his brother to turn his back to the mountains; then he moved the mountains right against this brother's back. When the Good Spirit told him he could turn around and look, the Bad Spirit bashed his nose against the mountain, and a crooked nose has characterized his appearance ever since.

The Bad Spirit pleaded with his brother not to kill him. His wish was granted, but only on the condition that he would serve henceforth to help take care of human beings. Consequently the Seneca and other Iroquoian peoples have societies that prepare masks used to impersonate the many forms of this bad brother; but their ritual acts are aimed at the cure of disease and the dispersion of witchcraft and other destructive agents.[6]

As reflected in this story, the Seneca hold an understanding of the character of the world and its creation markedly different from the Zuni. Certainly along with the Zuni, the Seneca (on the basis of this story) value those actions that conform to expectations. The brother who is born the proper way is the good brother. The brother who destroys his mother by bursting through her side in the improper way is a destroyer. The actions of the brothers distinguish their evaluation as good or bad, while at the same time they set the model for good and bad acts in human culture. The Seneca cosmology introduces the idea that even though such violations are clearly understood as bad, they nonetheless contribute to the shape and way of the world, as evidenced by the existence of pests, disease, death, and witchcraft. And the death of the mother is connected with the origination of staple foods. Instead of the Zuni search for that middle place where life forces are so delicately balanced that life-negating forces are nullified, the Seneca embrace those life-negating forces, institutionalizing them in the Society of Faces whose members wear the masks manifesting malevolent or bad entities, but for the effect of turning them, as in a mirror, back on themselves. The Society of Faces performs acts on the model of the Bad Spirit, but they do so in order to cure disease, fight witchcraft, and remove disorder. Comprehending the Seneca perspective on the power of the

Faces is unlikely without placing them in the framework of the Seneca cosmology and religious worldview.

Navajo: The Suffering Hero

Most Navajo stories tell of the heroes who lived in the mythic era after the world was created but before it was inhabited by the Navajo people. Many of these stories center on the adventures of the heroes, the consequences of their failures, and their resulting travail and misfortunes. The stories of heroes must be set in the context of the more pervasive world creation accounts.

Like their Zuni neighbors, the Navajo trace their origins from far beneath the present earth surface. They tell of four and sometimes more worlds stacked one on top of another below this earth-surface world. In these lower worlds, at a time before the Navajo world was given its present shape lived insect and animal people who acted in a manner resembling the present-day Navajo. The stories set in these lower worlds tell of strife, disorder, and confusion. No matter how hard these people tried, they could not stop fighting and committing wrongful acts like incest and adultery. As a result of their actions, each of the worlds on which they attempted to live was destroyed and they were forced to ascend to the next world level to find new places to live. As their forced journey of emergence progressed, the need became more and more urgent for a world in which all living things would know their proper places and live according to rules so that peace would prevail. Still the forces of disorder persisted with the rise of such things as witchcraft, disease, and all sorts of strife. The landscape of these lower worlds bore the barren character of the life patterns followed there.

Finally, fleeing the destruction of the lower worlds in which they lived, the people emerged onto the present earth surface, featureless and covered with water. With help, they succeeded in draining the water and drying the muds and those who had emerged planned that they would give form to this new world through ritual acts, performed first in a sweat lodge and then in a hogan (the name for the Navajo home, also used as a ceremonial place). Pieces of jewel from the medicine bundle of First Man were laid upon the floor to form a painting representing the various things that were planned to exist in the world. Features of the earth were shown, as well as its plant and animal life. Then, in a magical act of prayer, song, and breath, this representation of the world was transformed into the actual world, *dinetáh* or Navajoland. The creation hogan was itself a living form whose support pillars were the creators, whom the Navajo refer to as *diyin dine'é* or holy people, who hold up the sky. Though a hogan may appear rude in form and construction, its dome shape and earthen floor bear the basic structure of the cosmos.

The principle of order followed in these acts of creation was one of creating complementary pairs and placing the members across from one another so that they balance on the rim of the emergence place. The world, for example, is bounded by four mountains, which are also perceived as deities. These mountains stand at the four corners of the world, marking the cardinal directions, each having associated attributes similar to those described for the Zuni.

The creation of the earth surface produced a world in which everything was complemented and placed so as to balance on the center emergence place. When complete, the deities identified as the life forms of dawn and evening twilight were sent on a tour of all the mountains to inspect the creation. As they proceeded from one vantage point to another they found everything in place, in Navajo terms, the very definition of beauty (hózhó).

It is this world that Navajo heroes, characters rather like primordial humans, enter, a world in which everything exists in its proper place and with everything delicately balanced on a fulcrum at the center of the world, the emergence place. The heroism of these figures lies in the courage that enabled them to meet the requirement of living and moving about in this world so delicately balanced—for the very living of life leads to a disturbance of this world of beauty and threatens its collapse into chaos.[7] This cosmic drama is reflected in the adventures and plight of these heroes. A brief account will illustrate.

A young man traveling with his family departed by himself for a hunting trip to supply them with food. During his trip, he met a beautiful young woman, and they visited with each other. He became fond of her and spent the night, during which they had sexual contact. She neglected to tell him until later that she was the wife of White Thunder. The next morning, the youth continued his hunt and eventually killed a mountain sheep. He observed that its left horn bore the mark of zigzag lightning, and its left eye was missing. He ignored this omen of the wrath of White Thunder and butchered the animal, preparing to take the meat back to his family. But the sky clouded over, and it began to rain. The hunter took refuge under a spruce tree, keeping his arrows with him for protection. While he waited there, lightning struck the ground all around him. Each time, he heard a voice in the sky say, "He has not yet been struck. He does not lay his arrows aside!" The hunter wondered at this and, curious to see what would happen, he set his arrows against the tree. White Thunder was then able to get past the hunter's magical protection and in an instant struck the hunter with lightning, shattering him beyond recognition. Nothing was left of him but a streak of blood.

When the hunter failed to return, his family went in search of him. They found out what had happened and were told that only Gila Monster could help them. When they contacted Gila Monster, he demonstrated his powers of restoration by cutting himself up and scattering his various parts broadly about. These parts were gathered together, reassembled, and restored to life, all according to his powers and knowledge. Gila Monster then restored the hunter to life in a ceremonial that used this same knowledge and power. The ritual of restoration served not only to restore life to the hunter, but initiated him into the knowledge and powers of Gila Monster. This heroic adventure then gave origin to the Navajo tradition of ceremonial restoration known as Flintway, one of the ways by which Navajos bring order to a situation threatened by chaos, death, and disease.[8]

This story follows a common scenario for the whole genre of Navajo hero stories. The heroes, invariably in the process of a journey, enter forbidden territories or violate some regulation often unknown to them. As a consequence, they suffer in any number of ways, even to almost complete annihilation. When the heroes are unable to get out of their predicaments, others who possess special powers come to aid and relieve their suffering by performing ceremonials that restore them and also initiate the heroes into specific ritual knowledge.

Whereas the Navajo eras of creation were principally concerned with establishing proper places and relationships among everything in the world, the era of these heroes is concerned more with how one lives in the world. It deals with the boundaries of both places and relationships, with the relationships necessary for life, such as those between hunter and game, between husband and wife and women not his wife, between in-laws, between the living and the dead, between Navajos and non-Navajos, between a person and the plants and animals in the environment, and between human beings and deities. The effect of these stories is to define the Navajo way of life by testing limits and by reinforcing those limits through the adventures of the suffering heroes. The stories also provide insight into the vast and complex system of Navajo ritual focusing on health and healing.

Stories as Maps of Cultural Values

Not only Native Americans, but also humans generally, conceive and express the nature of the world as they understand it in the temporal and spatial terms of place or territory. Indeed it is valuation of place—that is, time and space—designations that gives orientation to all cultural and religious forms and sets the terms by which life is meaningfully lived. It is important to see beyond initial confusion and disbelief in what may appear as the fanciful character of Native American stories; for they map the perspectives and worldviews that make each culture distinct.

Notably, in comparing the three examples provided, there are certain similarities but also major distinctions. It is no simple exercise to understand this valuation of place for even one Native American culture. For all three cultures, the character of place takes shape in terms of how the culture is able to resolve the conflicting needs for a clearly defined sense of place—that is, rules and boundaries that define all human actions—and for unbounded freedom unfettered by rules or boundaries. In all three cases, the character of well-defined rules and boundaries is established not by dogmatism, but by acknowledging and often incorporating the creative powers of infringement upon proper place. This violation or infringement is also not confined to some story set in the primordial era of heroes, it has been incorporated into many religious practices and ceremonial performances. Contrary to the way they are often romantically and simplistically presented, Native American views of reality are not static structures in which reality is simply divided, for example, into four parts corresponding with the cardinal coordinates. Reality includes many dynamic and conflicting elements that are inseparable from human life. Native Americans, as people in all cultures, embody the struggle with the nature of human existence both in the content and form of their stories and through their rituals and ordinary ways of life.

THE TRICKSTER

While stories set "in the beginning" deal with fundamental values, categories, and relationships, so too, yet in markedly different ways, do stories about disruption, violation, and chaos. These stories explore the consequences of chaos and disorder, or simply a world without design. The human desire to be free of rules, to be unbound by time, space, or society, is dramatically and often humorously played out in many Native American cultures in the stories of a character commonly referred to as the trickster.[9] This figure is practically unnamable and undefinable. With a possible exception of being almost invariably male, his character is free of any of those restricting elements that give something definition and thus a name. It seems that the only dependable characteristic for the trickster is that he defies clear definition. In many Native American cultures, the trickster takes the form of a coyote, but a very unusual coyote. In some cultures, he has no particular form and can transform himself into any number of appearances. He is, in any case, the subject of numerous stories told throughout native North America, and this figure must be considered in terms of the valued distinctions of place and territory. Trickster stories are told much more often than stories of the creation of the world and they usually include children as well as adults in the audience. Clearly, for many Native Americans, trickster stories introduce and define elements of the worldview.

The flavor of trickster stories is shown in the well-known story of Eye-juggler. One Cheyenne account goes like this:

> There was a man who could send his eyes out of his head to a limb of a tree, and they would come back when called. Trickster ("White Man" is the Cheyenne name) wanted to do this, and he learned how from the man. But he was warned that he could do it no more than four times in one day. Trickster liked to do this because of the vantage he gained, but he paid no attention to the warning. One day when he sent his eyes out for the fifth time, he sent them to the highest tree he could find; but when he called them to return, they didn't. He called and waited and called and waited, but they didn't come back. Flies gathered on them as they started to spoil.
>
> Trickster lay on the ground unable to see and waited for something to happen. Soon a mouse approached and crawled on Trickster to snip a piece of hair for its nest. Trickster was thus able to catch it and force it to lead him around. The mouse pleaded to be released but wasn't let go until it gave Trickster one of its eyes. Trickster could then see, but the mouse's eye was so small that it went far back into Trickster's eye socket.

> Trickster then saw a buffalo grazing nearby. He told the buffalo his trouble and began to cry. The buffalo pitied him and gave him one of its eyes, but it was so large that it wouldn't go into Trickster's eye socket.[10]

This story is told many ways and can be made to apply to innumerable specific incidents, but there is a general lesson taught through the trickster's experience: one suffers the consequences of ignoring restrictions or rules.

In other trickster stories it is his sexual urges that remain unbounded. The Winnebago tell a story of a trickster who had such a long penis that he had to carry it coiled up in a box on his back.

> One day he went down to a lake and saw a number of girls swimming on the opposite shore. Attempting to use the advantage of his long penis, he dispatched it across the lake, but it tended to float. After several attempts at weighting it with rocks so it would go at the proper depth, he successfully lodged it in the chief's daughter. Various people were called to try to help the girl get free of this thing, but they didn't know what it was and couldn't help her. Finally an old woman was found who knew the ways of Trickster. She stood astride Trickster's penis and gouged it with an awl. Trickster pulled his penis back so quickly that the old woman was thrown a great distance.[11]

A plains version of this story places Trickster across a prairie from the women. The resolution comes when a herd of buffalo stampede between Trickster and the women, cutting his penis to its present size. The trod-upon pieces were then transformed into the animals of the prairie.

The utopian urges expressed in Trickster—his urges to be unbound and without limitations—often deal with food, for his appetite is insatiable and he never works for what he eats. This is featured in a Menomini story of a trickster.

> Two blind men were moved across the lake from the rest of the people where they might be safer. They were provided with food, and a rope was stretched from their lodge to the lake so they could find their way to the water. Racoon came by one day and watched what was going on. Each day one blind man would cook while the other went for water, and the next day they would trade jobs. Their food looked good to Racoon, so he played a trick on them in order to get some. When it was time to eat, one blind man started to cook the meat while the other went for water, but Racoon had moved the rope from the lake and tied it to a bush. The blind man who went for water returned distressed by the fact that the lake had dried up and that they would die without water. Racoon then replaced the rope, and when the other blind man went to try finding water, he found the lake and got water. While this was taking place, Racoon placed himself in the lodge and waited for the meat to be cooked. Eight pieces were prepared and placed between the two blind men. Racoon took four and started eating them while he watched what happened. Each of the blind men began to accuse the other of taking more than his share, and when their tempers were at a high pitch, Racoon slapped them both in

the face, thus making each think that the other had done it. While they rolled about fighting, Racoon took the rest of the food and laughed out loud as he left. The men stopped fighting when they realized what had happened, and Racoon told them they should learn not to find fault with each other so easily.[12]

An Apache version of this story concerns Coyote and two blind women. It ends with Coyote inflicting a cruel death on the two women.[13]

Trickster is an important figure in the oral traditions of many Native American people. From these several examples it is perhaps clear why. Trickster embodies the human struggle against the confinement felt by being bound to place, even within the obvious necessity of such definition in order to prevent chaos. In many of his adventures, Trickster permits people to vicariously experience the thrills and freedoms of a utopian existence. But his folly reveals the very meaning of the boundaries and relationships between bounded places that give order to human life. Undoubtedly, the fun and exciting, even gross and risqué, aspects of these stories contributes to their attractiveness and effectiveness, but it is certainly clear that, to Native American people, these stories have far more significance than simple entertainment, the status consigned to them by most interpretive studies.

STRUCTURES OF REALITY
IN ARCHITECTURE AND ART

The temporal and spatial distinctions people of any culture use to construct and negotiate their world are usually easily discernable in Native American cultures. Stories provide natural language articulation of these valued distinctions but they are also made in other cultural forms. They are found in social structure, in mythic geography, and in architecture. The village of Zuni replicates the cosmic pattern, as do the Navajo hogan and ancestral lands. In many Native American cultures landscapes, villages, ceremonial grounds, ceremonial lodges, and common homes replicate the form and process of their world. An unfortunate tendency among observers of Native American cultures, including scholars, has been to collapse the many distinctive cultural value systems imprinted on categories and relationships articulated in terms of place, to a single oversimplified pattern, usually a sacred circle, presented as common to all Native American cultures. This is not accurate.

The appreciation of the complexity of the cosmic symbolism that can be borne by architectural forms is enhanced in a brief examination of the significance of the temporal and spatial organization of the Delaware/Lenape Big House. The term Big House refers both to a ceremony and the structure in which it takes place. From the Delaware/Lenape point of view, the religion of the Big House stems from the origin of the world, and they feel that all other religions have emerged from it.

The lodge is built with four walls covered by a partial roof open in the center, through which extends the center pole erected in the lodge floor. The lodge bears cosmic symbolism in its equation of the floor with the earth, the walls with the four quarters of the world, and the roof with the vault of the sky. On the center post is carved the face image of *mesi'ŋgok,* the creator and supreme power. The lodge centers on this figure, as does the religion. The pole rooted in the earth pierces the sky through the twelve levels that form the abode of *mesi'ŋgok.* He holds the top of the pole in his hand. Faces carved on the support pillars on each wall represent the *manitou,* or spirits, of these cosmic regions.

The lodge has doors on the east and west that are associated, respectively, with the rising sun, symbol of the beginning of things, and the setting sun, symbol of the end of things. Beneath the earthen floor are the underworlds.

The prescribed ritual order of movement in the lodge requires entrance through the east door, movement in a circular direction to the north around the center pole, and exit through the west door. This movement pattern represents the cycle of life, the white path. Within the lodge are specified places for people in the three clan groupings—wolf, turtle, and turkey—and for the men who sit apart from the women.

The Big House ceremony ritually enacts transit through the year. It transpires over twelve nights, representing the twelve moons or lunar months of the year. The dancing that follows the white path symbolizes the east-to-west movement of the sun as well as the passage of life from birth to death.

This is but the most simple description of the valued place distinctions of the Big House religion of the Delaware/Lenape. It is carried out in much greater detail and throughout the many smaller elements of the ritual dress, face painting, ritual paraphernalia, and ritual procedures.[14]

Importantly, the distinctive designation of place categories and relationships is the way the people of cultures create and negotiate reality. To be of a culture, to hold specific personal and cultural identity, is to know one's place, to know the territory.

Throughout native North America, cultural and religious values are also introduced through the artwork that is so intricate a part of clothing, utensils, masks, drums, and ritual objects. The well-known medicine pipe of the Sioux and other people bears the symbols of the plants, animals, birds, various domains of the universe, seasons, and history of the people, all of which are brought together with their counterparts in the spiritual world in the prayerful act of smoking the pipe.[15]

Through the aesthetic works of artisans a vision of the world held by Native Americans can be seen. The old tradition of Eskimo carving, done before the advent of tourist curio markets, was a process in which, in their terms, the carver (and all Eskimo men were carvers) saw and revealed the form that lay within the uncarved materials. The carver would hold the unworked piece of ivory, turning it in his hands, contemplating it until he could see what form lay within it. Carving was not considered to be a process of the artist conquering or commanding the raw materials to conform to his ideas. Rather it was a process of releasing the form already resident in the material.[16]

Evidence of this view is apparent in a dialogue between two contemporary Pacific Northwest Coast craftsmen, Bill Holm and Bill Reid, as they consider some old pipes. Reid speaks of the wood-carving process as being driven by a "crazy mystique of the object inside the wood." Holm agrees with this, "The artist has to see that form in there." Reid then says that the craftsman must have "the courage to take it [the carving] beyond the point your mind tells you is logical."[17] This view of reality, that sense of the shape of things, is not only in the visual objects, it is also a part of the process by which these objects are created. The process is not one of dogmatically applying form or structure to raw material or of consciously creating symbols to stand for one's ideas. It is an interrelational process of seeing that the principles and forms of reality, that is, the intentionalities these forms embody, are already present in all things, even in an uncarved piece of ivory or wood, even in the most common, everyday things.

COSMICIZATION OF THE ORDINARY

Religion, the religious, is often considered beyond or other than the ordinary. Religion occurs on holidays or Sundays and in special places. Yet, religion is also lived and practiced at the most banal levels of life. Lame Deer was a wily old Oglala when he and his white friend Richard Erdoes engaged in composing his biography. He had lived his long life during the most difficult period in the history of the people of the northern plains, a period characterized by the constant threat of complete collapse and loss of cultural identity. This did not greatly embitter Lame Deer, although he liked to take advantage of aspects of his culture to point up its richness against what he felt was the impoverished condition of European-American culture.

In a conversation with Erdoes, Lame Deer explains how the most common objects may reflect grand cosmic principles. It is a kind of meditation on a soot-covered cooking pot.

> What do you see here, my friend? Just an ordinary old cooking pot, black with soot and full of dents.
>
> It is standing on the fire on top of that old wood stove, and the water bubbles and moves the lid as the white steam rises to the ceiling. Inside the pot is boiling water, chunks of meat with bone and fat, plenty of potatoes.
>
> It doesn't seem to have a message, that old pot, and I guess you don't give it a thought . . .
>
> But I'm an Indian. I think about ordinary, common things like this pot. The bubbling water comes from the rain cloud. It represents the sky. The fire comes from the sun which warms us all—men, animals, trees. The meat stands for the four-legged creatures, our animal brothers, who gave of themselves so that we should live. The steam is living breath. It was water; now it goes up to the sky, becomes a cloud again. These things are sacred. Looking at that pot full of good soup, I am thinking how, in this simple

manner, Wakan Tanka takes care of me. We Sioux spend a lot of time thinking about everyday things, which in our mind are mixed up with the spiritual . . . We Indians live in a world of symbols and images where the spiritual and the commonplace are one . . . We try to understand them not with the head but with the heart, and we need no more than a hint to give us the meaning.

(Reprinted with the permission of Simon & Schuster Adult Publishing Group from *Lame Deer: Seeker of Visions* by John (Fire) Lame Deer and Richard Erdoes. Copyright © 1972 by John (Fire) Lame Deer and Richard Erdoes.)

Meaningful visual patterns commonly appear in Native American art, architecture, songs, prayers, stories, and ritual processes. One of these motifs related to the Navajo example presented earlier can be explained.

Recall that in Navajo hero stories there is often tension between a static, balanced order that characterizes the state of perfect beauty and the necessary disruption of that order and beauty as a part of the life process. The dynamic character of that tension is reflected in the iconic motif of the incomplete circle, which is ubiquitous in Navajo culture. Its most common incidence is as a circular enclosure with an opening or doorway, as in the Navajo hogan and sweatlodge. It appears in both the design and coil construction of Navajo baskets, in the incised design that encircles the neck of Navajo pottery jars, in the pathway or opening in the border designs of Navajo weaving, and in the encircling guardian of a sandpainting. Movement within a hogan, especially during ceremonies, occurs in a pattern that prevents complete or closed circles.

The open circle nonetheless constitutes a boundary. It sets off a space and gives it significance. The break or opening that is the most distinctive aspect of the motif serves in a pragmatic sense as an orientation device. That position is the one to be aligned with the east or to define the direction east. It is the point to which all other points are related. But at another level, Navajo people consider the opening as a pathway leading out of the enclosed space. It is always seen as the road out, and this road is the road of life. Navajos say that to draw a closed circle around someone's house will cause sickness, perhaps even death because it is an obstruction of the out-going life road.

A Navajo funerary custom uses this motif to articulate Navajo values. If a person dies in a hogan, the body is not carried out the door, for carrying it along the road of life would be highly inappropriate. Consequently, the body is removed through a hole knocked in the north side of the hogan. This also ruins the house for any further habitation. It is abandoned and avoided.

This iconic motif of the open circle visually bears the concepts central to those stories. These concepts can be summarized as follows: The world was created in perfect beauty, but perfect beauty means a static order. Because life is a dynamic process requiring movement, it risks destroying this beauty. So as disorder arises and life is threatened, one must be able to reconstitute order and beauty in the world. This is done by the ritual re-creation of the pattern of perfect beauty.

The Navajo way of life is a process of moving from a domain of perfect beauty into history, the threat of chaos motivates a return to ritual in order to achieve re-creation and renewal. Navajo life can be portrayed as a pathway out of the domain of the perfect beauty of fresh creation into history, into the profane world. But it also provides a way in which even disorder and the threatening aspects of life may be seen as meaningful, real, and necessary. The pathway through the opening in the circle shows that the space inside and the space outside, the time of story and the time of humans in history, the world of beauty and order and the world of ugliness and disorder, are intimately interdependent. It shows that the cosmic processes occur in the individual and that the sufferings of the individual are part of cosmic processes. The ubiquitous open circle represents and enacts this fundamental element in the Navajo worldview.

CONCLUSION

This chapter shows that an important approach to understanding any aspect of Native American religions is to comprehend as fully as possible the culture's worldview, that broadest framework which gives shape not only to the whole of reality, but is also used to negotiate the exigencies of every aspect of mundane life. Evidence of this worldview can be found most immediately in stories, especially stories that tell of the creation of the world—for in the process of creation, the world is given its broadest order and shape. Since everything in the material world has the culturally designated attributes of time and space, anything can bear these marks of cultural value. Literally, anything can be a symbol of a culture's understanding of the shape of reality or some aspect of it.

The examples presented also show that no generally applicable Native American view of reality exists and that the many diverse views are complex and sophisticated. It is especially important to see that Native American views of reality are not at all static. Among the examples considered, none express the view that religious and cultural significance is limited to a rigidly defined place. Native American worldviews often bestow a certain creative power and therefore place, within even religious practice and belief to the acts that violate order. Hence disease, death, trespass, witchcraft, and the like are all matters of religious significance even though they are not given a positive value. The Seneca Bad Spirit, the trickster, the trespassing Navajo heroes all are vitally important to the articulation of a valued reality. Consequently, they are meaningful religious figures. They embody the struggles and dynamics of being human.

NOTES

1. Ruth L. Bunzel, *Introduction to Zuni Ceremonialism,* Smithsonian Institution, Bureau of American Ethnology, 47th Annual Report (Washington, D.C., 1929), p. 481.

2. See the following for the creation mythology of the Zuni: Ruth L. Bunzel, "Zuni Texts," *Publications of the American Ethnological Society* 15 (1933); Frank H. Cushing, *Outline of*

Zuni Creation Myths, Smithsonian Institute, Bureau of American Ethnology, 13th Annual Report (Washington, D.C., 1896), pp. 325–447; E.C. Parsons, "The Origin Myth of Zuni," *Journal of American Folklore* 36 (1923): 135–62; and Dennis Tedlock, *Finding the Center: Narrative Poetry of the Zuni Indians* (New York: Dial, 1972).

3. Frank H. Cushing, *Outline of Zuni Creation Myths,* pp. 367–73.

4. For a discussion of the significance of this issue in the study of religion, see Jonathan Z. Smith, *Map Is Not Territory* (Leiden: E. J. Brill, 1979), especially the essays "The Influence of Symbols on Social Change: A Place on Which to Stand," pp. 129–46; and "Map Is Not Territory," pp. 289–310; and Sam Gill, "Territory" in *Critical Terms for Religious Sudies.* Edited by Mark C. Taylor. Chicago: University of Chicago Press, 1998, pp. 298–313.

5. For studies of the earth-diver-type myth, see Alan Dundes, "Earth Diver: Creation of the Mythopoeic Male," *American Anthropologist* 64 (1962): 1032–51; and Elli Kaija Kongas, "The Earth-Diver (Th. A812)," *Ethnohistory* 7 (1960): 151–80.

6. This story is based on the version reported in A. F. C. Wallace, *The Death and Rebirth of the Seneca* (New York: Vantage, 1969), pp. 86–91.

7. For a discussion of the general structure and themes of Navajo mythology, see Sam D. Gill, *Songs of Life: An Introduction to Navajo Religious Culture* (Leiden: E. J. Brill, 1979).

8. Father Berard Haile, *Origin Legend of the Navaho Flintway* (Chicago: University of Chicago Press, 1943).

9. Kimberly A. Christen, *Clowns and Tricksters: An Encyclopedia of Tradition and Culture* (Denver: ABC-CLIO, 1998).

10. This story is based on the account recorded by Alfred Kroeber, "Cheyenne Tales," *Journal of American Folklore* 13 (1900): 168.

11. This is based on the story in Paul Radin, *The Trickster* (New York: Schocken, 1956), pp. 19–20.

12. Walter J. Hoffman, *The Menomini Indians,* Bureau of American Ethnology, 14th Annual Report (Washington, D.C., 1896), p. 211.

13. Morris Opler, *Myths and Legends of the Lipan Apache Indians* (New York: American Folklore Society, 1942), p. 185.

14. For further details, see Frank G. Speck, *A Study of the Delaware Big House Ceremony* (Harrisburg: Pennsylvania Historical Commission, 1931); Frank G. Speck, *The Celestial Bear Comes Down To Earth* (Reading, Pa.: Reading Public Museum and Art Gallery, 1945); and Mark R. Harrington, "Religion and Ceremonies of the Lenape," *Indian Notes and Monographs* (New York: Museum of the American Indian, Heye Foundation, 1921).

15. For a description of the prayerful act of smoking the pipe, see Joseph Epes Brown, ed., *The Sacred Pipe* (Norman: University of Oklahoma Press, 1953), Chapter 1.

16. Edmund Carpenter, *Eskimo Realities* (New York: Holt, Rinehart and Winston, 1973), p. 59.

17. Bill Holm and Bill Reid, *Indian Art of the Northwest Coast* (Seattle: University of Washington Press, 1975), p. 36.

3

Orality and Native American Religions

Among the Omaha, it was a custom at the funeral of a highly respected man or woman for several youths to make two incisions in their upper left arms which they kept open by inserting a willow twig. With blood dripping from their wounds, as an expression of their grief, they danced before the lodge that housed the dead and sang songs with blithe major cadences suggesting birds, sunshine, and lightness. This practice bears the Omaha belief that song is capable of carrying human thoughts and aspirations beyond the human world. The songs of the youths cheer the dead as he or she goes into the world beyond.[1]

Native Americans commonly view songs, prayers, stories, and other oral events as manifesting powerful forces. Certain words when spoken or sung affect the world, give it shape and meaning. Words can cause pain and suffering as well as create beauty and orderliness.

In several Pueblo stories of creation, the first figure to exist—who, in a sense, has always existed—was Thought-Woman. The world was literally formed as she thought what form it should take. Her partners in creation followed her act of creative thinking by naming those things given form by Thought-Woman. Thus, her acts of creation became humanly meaningful through language. Names gave distinction and identity to the forms created.[2]

In Central California, thought and speech are personified as the cosmic creators. Many of the creation stories feature a figure who creates the world as he thinks of it or speaks about it. This figure is countered by Coyote, a sort of trickster, whose acts undo or reverse the way the world is created. In this way, the difficult aspects of the human plight, including death, are introduced. The story is similar to the Seneca tale of the Twin Brothers. For the Achomawi of California, thought and speech are independent creators, as evident in their creation story.

> Apponahah speaks and sings to himself, in his own mind, and thus imagines himself to be the creator of the world. But in the first conversation between Apponahah and Annikadel, who is the personification of speech and was carried as a child in the bosom of Apponahah, Annikadel declares his role in creation by telling Apponahah that thought alone is insufficient as a creator; that thought must be born into the world and that this requires an act of speech. Annikadel proclaims himself as "a man of the air," as "the man who will make all sounds," and thus as the partner of thought in creation. He even declares that he made Apponahah think of all that he had done, thus indicating the dependence even of thought on speech.[3]

In the Navajo stories of creation, similar roles are played by thought and speech.

> After the people who were to perform the acts of creation emerged from lower worlds onto the mud-covered earth surface, there was a display of the forces that would create life on that surface. It was done by the personification of the objects in the medicine bundle, the womb of life. From the bundle arose a youth and a maiden of incomparable beauty. Their hair was long, and their bodies shone brilliantly. They appeared only this one brief time on earth, but they revealed that they were the means by which all things would be given life; they were to be the very means of life.[4]

The youth and maiden are the personifications of thought and speech, and their names are Long Life and Happiness. Joined together, they comprise the force that carries life through time. Even their names are used together by the Navajo as a term that designates the goal of life. All Navajo prayers and songs evoke the names Long Life and Happiness *(sa'áh naghai bik'eh hózhó),* for thought and speech are the forces necessary to create life and maintain the conditions and means by which people live in good health through a long life to attain fulfillment by death in old age.

In these examples, the acts of thought and speech, though playing an array of valued roles, are of special religious significance to many Native American people. The creative power of the word is reminiscent of the passage in Christian scripture in the Book of John: "In the beginning was the Word. . . ."

Until the application of linguists' orthographic (i.e., writing) systems, Native American languages had never been written. A system of writing was also introduced by the Cherokee man Sequoya in 1821. At present, few Native Americans read their own languages, although some cultures like the Navajo and Hopi have developed a considerable literature published in their own languages. The modes of communication used by cultures importantly shape aspects of their way of life. Because the whole academic enterprise and the modern Western world highly value writing, it is tempting to think of

Native Americans as preliterate or illiterate or, to try to be less judgmental, as nonliterate. Still these are negative terms, even if positively intended, focusing on what Native Americans do not do or do not have. It is an easy step from here to denigrate or romanticize them. Perhaps a little better term is exclusively oral, though inelegant and even in its positive, the statement is still rooted in the negative. On so many of these matters the awkwardness continually reminds us that Western and outsider perspectives with their built in values can never be fully set aside.

How is it possible to understand and appreciate the importance of Native American modes of communication without either denigrating them with the implications of terms like illiterate or romanticizing them with terms like preliterate? No small imagination is required to appreciate and gain a feeling for the character of exclusively oral cultures. The consideration of Native American examples will initiate this act of imagination as well as correct certain likely erroneous associations.

TO BREATHE IS TO MAKE POETRY

In the Amassalik Eskimo language, the word for "to breathe" is the same as the word for "to make poetry," and it stems from the word referring to the soul or force of life. The Netsilik group of Eskimo have the same idea, as shown in comments made by the man named Orpingalik. He was a great hunter, archer, kayakman, and religious leader or shaman. As a shaman, he could engage in the world beyond the human with the aid of spirit helpers and guides who had chosen him. He communicated with the spirit world, or it communicated through him, by entering a state of trance. He called his spirits and spoke with them by singing their songs and by speaking in the special metaphorical language of Netsilik shamans. His powers gave him the capability to see game and to hunt successfully, to heal as well as to injure his enemies. He could call the caribou to him through the power of his songs.

> Wild caribou, land louse, long legs,
> With the great ears,
> And the rough hairs on your neck,
> Flee not from me.
> Here I bring skins for soles,
> Here I bring moss for wicks,
> Just come gladly
> Hither to me, hither to me.[5]

Orpingalik's songs and poetry were the base for his success as a hunter and a measure of his stature as a human being. His food as well as his dignity was inseparable from his songs. The Eskimo consider a person's songs as his or her property and no one would perform the song or poem of another without permission and compensation for it.

Orpingalik spoke provocatively of songs.

> How many songs I have I cannot tell you. I keep no count of such things.
> There are so many occasions in one's life when a joy or a sorrow is felt in
> such a way that the desire comes to sing; and so I only know that I have
> many songs. All my being is song, and I sing as I draw breath. . . . It is
> just as necessary for me to sing as it is to breathe.[6]

This identification of song with the riches of life is addressed in the poignant
statement of a Navajo man, "I have always been a poor man. I do not know a
single song."[7]

To make song is an act of vitality no less than to breathe. To sing is rooted
in the heart, the seat of life and center of emotions. To sing is not only a sign
of life, but, as importantly, an act of life. It is creative in the most primary
sense. Orpingalik spoke eloquently of this.

> Songs are thoughts, sung out with the breath when people are moved by
> great forces and ordinary speech no longer suffices.
>   Man is moved just like the ice floe sailing here and there out in the
> current. His thoughts are driven by a flowing force when he feels joy,
> when he feels fear, when he feels sorrow. Thoughts can wash over him like
> a flood, making his breath come in gasps and his heart throb. Something,
> like an abatement in the weather, will keep him thawed up. And then it will
> happen that we, who always think we are small, will feel still smaller. And we
> will fear to use words. But it will happen that the words we need will come
> of themselves. When the words we want to use shoot up of themselves—we
> get a new song.[8]

There is great depth in Orpingalik's view. Singing glib songs of joy to celebrate a life of bliss that is never actually realized by human beings is not the
song he is referring to. Rather it is the songs that are concerned with the measure of life with all its complexities and overwhelming difficulties. The mind
only grasps life's meaning as it finds a vehicle of expression and manifestation
in words, songs, and poetry.

Only these forms can capture a measure of the incomparable sadness of a
mother who loses her son because he has been banished from the community
after he accidentally killed a hunting companion, as happened in Orpingalik's
family. The poem that came to Orpingalik's wife, Uvlunuaq, arose from this
event.

> When message came
> Of the killing and the flight,
> Earth became like a mountain with pointed peak,
> And I stood on the awl-like pinnacle
> And faltered,
> And fell![9]

Owners of powerful words are themselves often powerful and prestigious
in their cultures, but they are also subject to the suspicions of community

members when anything goes wrong. Because powerful persons can engage in religious actions that have powerful effects, they are suspect when something goes awry, even when they are the only ones who suffer. Often the only thing that distinguishes sorcerers and malevolent beings from shamanic healers and clairvoyants is the intent or nature of their effects on the world. The powers of one who can bring the dead back to life, heal the ill, or call the animals are dangerously close to those of the sorcerer whose curse or spell can cause illness, deprivation, or even death. The death of another of Orpingalik's sons was judged by the people of his community to have resulted from Orpingalik's attempts to use his powers to kill a rival shaman. They said that the powers of the rival were thus proven the stronger because the efforts of Orpingalik were reflected back upon him, killing his son in an accident.[10]

Perhaps at this point, efforts to appreciate the strong interconnection among thoughts, words, and life and the distinctive character of speech acts may be aided by a general and naive comparison of oral and written modes of communication.

Speech is an act that is fragile, impermanent, and intimate. Every speech act is unique, engaging a speaker and a listener in a specific existential situation. All that transpires is the formation of words, symbols of sound, stemming from thoughts. When uttered by the mouth in an act that requires the expiration of breath, these thoughts fill the surrounding space within the power of the sounds. The listeners, including the speaker, receive the sounds through their ears. There remains nothing of the speech act except the impressions it leaves in the memories and effects it renders upon the world. Speech by its nature is personal. It cannot occur other than from person to person, from speaker to listener. It is an act of the mouth, breath, heart, ear, and mind. Speech is of the body. A speech event cannot be audited, replayed, or reorganized. There is a limited capacity for recall even in the memory it produces.

Communication in writing is quite different. Writing certainly stems from the mind and often the heart, but it is an act of the hand, usually produced less spontaneously and more slowly and laboriously, because a system of alphabetic symbols must be engaged to translate the stream of mental symbols into visual images. For this price, however, the written message may be audited, corrected, or erased before it need be submitted to a receiver, a reader. And the reader may reread, reorder, and rephrase it without loss of the original message.

Writing and reading are usually private acts, done by oneself in isolation from others. Reading is physically more directed than is listening. One may much more easily choose to read something than to hear something. Sight is also greatly directed by the viewer, who changes the direction of vision and focuses according to desire. It is said that persons who are blind until adulthood, then given eyesight by an operation, cannot at first discern one object from another but see only a complex configuration of shapes. This is because they have not yet learned how to look, how to direct the vision toward the desired centers of attention.

Acts of writing are not as fragile as are speech acts. Whatever one writes is more or less stable, permanent, and can be read at any time by anyone who knows how to read the language. Negatively, as anyone who has written secret notes in school knows, there is less control on who receives the message. Once it is written, neither the intended receivers nor the context in which the message is intended to be read can always be controlled.

Although these points are fundamental and reveal no new information, to recount them will develop a perspective from which to understand some aspects of Native American religions shaped by exclusive orality.

THE COCK AND THE MOUSE

The oral poetry of Native Americans is often described as stable in its form and composition. Until recently, folklorists approached the collection of stories, songs, and prayers in Native American cultures largely with the attitude of checking the occurrence of a certain type of tale or song in an effort to record the lore and oral poetry of a particular culture. Variations of a tale or song were usually not considered as separate incidents and they were reconciled by putting all of the versions together to form an abstract of what was then considered as the complete story. This approach tends to give the impression that each Native American people had a fixed tradition of poetry and that actual performance of it was always some corruption or extraction of the full form. Many folklorists have also documented the stability of various forms of oral poetry over long periods of time. Others have shown that many forms—such as origin stories, songs, and especially prayers—are highly formal and their exact recitation is often rigidly followed.

The measure of flexibility, innovation, and creativity can be shown by considering an incident that occurred during the late nineteenth century at Zuni. Frank H. Cushing, an ethnographer, listened to several Zuni men tell folk tales during the summer of 1886. The custom was for everyone to contribute stories in turn. When Cushing's turn came to tell a story, he had to resort to tales that had their roots in Europe. On one occasion, he told them the tale of "the cock and the mouse." A mouse asked a cock to go with him to collect some nuts from a nearby tree. The mouse climbed the tree to gather the nuts, but the cock was unable to fly up to the tree and asked the mouse to throw him a nut. When the mouse did so, the nut hit the cock, breaking open his head. The remainder of the story is a chain of events in which the cock must go to a series of sources in order to cure his head. The total series comes at the end, when the fountain gave the cock some water, which he gave to the forest, which gave him wood, which he gave to the baker, who gave him bread, which he gave to the dog, who gave him two hairs, which he gave to the old woman, who gave him some rags, which the cock needed to cure his head. This tale was then unknown to the Zuni.

Cushing returned to the Zuni about a year later. One day in a similar session of telling tales, Cushing heard his own story of a year earlier told by a Zuni. Cushing's recording of the story enables the examination of the changes it underwent during the period of a single year. While the basic tale remained intact, the story was adapted to Zuni culture and worldview. The Zuni story was more than fivefold the length of the tale told by Cushing. The Zuni developed a more complicated relationship between the mouse and the cock and they added many details to give the story concrete images associated with Zuni life ways. The conclusion of the story exemplifies this process of adaptation. When the cock reaches the source of water, a spring, the spirit of water had a message for him.

> Long have men neglected their duties, and the Beloved of the Clouds need payment of due no less than ourselves, the Trees, the Food-maker, the Dog, and the Old Woman. Behold! no plumes [prayer feathers] are set about our border! Now, therefore, pay to them of thy feathers—four floating plumes from under thy wings—and set them close over us, that, seen in our depths from the sky, they will lure the Beloved of the Clouds with their rain-laden breaths. Thus will our streamway be replenished and the Trees watered, and their Winds in the Trees will drop the dead branches wherewith thou mayest make payment and all will be well.
>
> Forthwith the *Tákaka* [the cock] plucked four of his best plumes and set them, one on the northern, one on the western, one on the southern, and one on the eastern border of the Pool. Then the Winds of the Four Quarters began to breathe upon the four plumes, and with those Breaths of the Beloved came Clouds, and from the Clouds fell Rain. . . .[11]

Thus, the cock was able to get the bristles from the dog so that grandmother would cure his head. The Zuni see opportunity in the story to recount the origin of various things in the Zuni world. For example, the head injury gave origin to the red fleshy cock's comb. The practice by which each party required payment for what it gave coincides with a medicine master requiring payment for his services and medicines; there is no virtue in medicine of no value.

What this Zuni example illustrates is the potential of oral traditions to adapt to the specific cultural needs and circumstances. In only one year, the telling and retelling of a new tale was thoroughly adapted to the Zuni worldview and made to bear a number of messages regarding proper action, proper conduct, the interrelationship among all living things, the dependence of life on spiritual levels of reality, and the dependence of life on proper religious actions. Folklorists have warned that it is naive to consider that any folktale has a specific meaning for a culture that tells it. They note that one can find the same basic tale, such as "the cock and the mouse," in many cultures. But, while the basic elements of this tale remain the same, clearly in this example it has been greatly adapted to Zuni culture and religion.

This example provides background for the consideration of various factors involved in the transmission of culture. Many objects in material culture play a vital role in the transmission of culture, yet speech acts are important and, because they can be interpreted and translated, provide access to outsiders. In cultures without written records, the whole history and character of the tradition must be maintained in the memories of its living members. Culture is transmitted in acts of face-to-face communication, a chain of interlocking conversations. Every member of an exclusively oral culture must personally and directly experience the tradition because it is largely transmitted in verbal acts. The relationship between words and their meanings is experienced directly and concretely. Tradition is highly socialized because it is communicated only between people through social interaction.

Because the whole of tradition must be held in the memory, cultures commonly adopt various devices to aid the task of remembering. Certain processes are inseparable from the oral transmission of culture. The forms of speech themselves—stories, songs, and prayers—as well as requirements for the exact recitation of certain speech acts serve to shield the memory from extensive change due to influences of the immediate present. Yet, while remembering is essential, forgetting nonetheless serves to eliminate from the tradition anything that becomes irrelevant or meaningless. Only what is humanly relevant is retained in the memory; the rest, in time, is forgotten. The processes of incorporating present experiences in the tradition corresponds with the elimination of details through forgetting. This dynamic transmission of culture, including the function of remembering and forgetting, can be viewed as a process of digestion. New elements are constantly being added, though these alter the whole character of cultural identity only very slowly in a growthlike process. But as the culture is fed by new experiences, certain aspects of tradition that have become irrelevant may be sloughed off by being forgotten. Yet, even the forgotten details retain an effect by having contributed to the ever-changing shape that distinguishes a culture.

Story is an ideal form for effecting this process of transmitting culture. Even the simple tale of the cock and the mouse has, as the Zuni example shows, almost unlimited potential for elaboration and development. It is notable also that the Zuni primordialize the story, thus giving it world-defining authority. This is also done in the etiological or explanatory elements at the story's end. To attribute to the story an explanation of how the cock got its comb, is a way of validating the story. Because it is evident that cocks have combs, it follows that the story is relevant to the Zuni world of experience.

The consideration of Native American stories is often driven by a desire to comprehend what they mean. Stories somehow are not adequately satisfying in their being heard. Sensing that stories are pregnant with meaning, there is an insatiable hunger for articulatable meaning. My experience has suggested that such an approach may not be fruitful. After spending much time asking Native American people questions like "What does this story mean?" and feeling, by their lack of response, that it must have been a stupid question—or having gained answers completely incompatible with the story—I have had to seek new ways of understanding how these stories bear meaning and how to best appreciate them. Surely any understanding of Native American religions will be lacking until this problem is considered.

Consider certain olfactory experiences. I cannot smell the odor of juniper smoke without it evoking a series of particular images and feelings related to experiences I had while living among Navajo people. If asked what the smell of juniper smoke means to me, I would at first be confounded, for such a question seems inappropriate. The smell bears no translatable message, although it has an emotional impact. The experience is full of meaning, but has no meaning at all in the sense of bearing a message. Listening to music often evokes similar sorts of meaning by awakening a certain emotion, often a series of images or memories connected with the music through one's personal and cultural history.

The speech acts in Native American cultures certainly convey information that can be discerned by familiarity with the language and its conventions. But these speech acts have an emotional impact, a significance much more far-reaching. In their performance, they are not simply streams of words whose full significance lies in the information they convey. They are complex symbols, networks of sounds that evoke odors, forms, colors, temperatures, and rhythms. All of these nonverbal features and many more create the patterns through which reality is perceived, by which cultural reality is created. They create the moods and goals that give orientation to life. They provide a presence in which actions take on value. Consequently, any story, any song, any prayer is a stimulus that frees strings of associated images, emotions, and patterns. The significance is inseparable from the whole experiential field they evoke. To ask what these speech acts mean and expect a translatable message or a simple explanation is almost always to ask an inappropriate question.

PERFORMANCE

So far I have said things about oral traditions in Native American cultures that may appear contradictory. I have contended that, from the Native American perspective, certain verbal utterances are creative acts of the highest order. But I have also maintained that the stories do not have their greatest meaning in terms of bearing abstractable messages. The notion of performance will help resolve the tension and give further insight into the nature of the oral aspects of culture that are so important to Native American religious traditions. Consider the Navajo prayer to the crane.

Dark Male Crane,
I have made a sacrifice to you!
Coming from the home of dark cloud, from the floor of dark cloud, from the square rooms of dark cloud, along the out-trail controlled by dark cloud, along the trail at the tip of dark cloud, you who travel along with the aid of dark cloud!

When you have come upon me by means of your feet of dark cloud you have thereby wholly restored my feet! *[Line repeated four times, changing feet to legs, body, mind, and voice.]*

May the power that enables you to inhale also enable me to inhale, may the power that enables you to exhale also enable me to exhale, may the power that enables you to utter a word also enable me to utter a word, may the power that enables you to speak also enable me to speak!

May the means that keep your feet in health also keep my feet in health! *[Line repeated four times, changing feet to legs, body, mind, and voice.]*

With its aid you have nicely made me whole again, you have perfectly restored me! You have put me back into my former condition! May you nicely raise me on my feet, do walk me out nicely!

May you cause me to walk about nicely!
May it be pleasant wherever I go!
May it always be pleasant at my front wherever I go!
May it always be pleasant in my rear wherever I go!
Pleasant again it has come to be, pleasant again it has come to be!

(Father Barard Haile, *Origin Legend of the Navaho Flintway,* 1943. Reprinted by permission of The University of Chicago Press.)

This prayer to the crane is repeated addressing several others: White Female Crane, Blue Male Crane, Sparkling Female Crane, Wind, Big Fly, Changing Woman, Sun Carrier, Pollen Boy, and Cornbeetle Girl. Appropriate changes are made for the corresponding house descriptions and related phenomena. The other prayers in this ritual process known as Flintway differ only in the names mentioned and the corresponding phenomena.

This prayer may be appreciated in a number of ways. It is aesthetically pleasing in its imagery, symmetry, and rhythms. It conveys relevant information about Navajo culture. The prayer apparently addresses Dark Male Crane in reference to a ritual sacrifice made to it, then describes the figure coming from its home. It then beseeches Dark Male Crane to restore the body of the one praying, concluding with a statement that the restoration has been accomplished and describing the pleasant experience of being restored. This summary may seem like a satisfactory understanding, but there is much more to it.

Knowledge of Native American religions usually comes to people seeking an academic understanding in the form of written texts, usually in collections of texts or in ethnographies. In written text presentations, the oral component is completely lost as is the original language. The text is stripped of the tradition, separated from its cultural context. In this form it can speak only to the reader's sense of meaning and value. Readers lack the perspective of those who live it. While an English-speaking Navajo who knows the quoted prayer might write it down, perhaps to appear just as I have presented it, this act of writing down a prayer has nothing to do with the performance of Navajo traditions. Writing prayers is not an act of the culture. The prayer, when performed as a religious act, is carefully placed in a ceremonial context according to an extensive set of rules. Indeed, Navajos do not recite the prayer outside of highly specified contexts. Clearly all cultures distinguish between talking about certain aspects of the culture's traditions and actually performing the acts as part of a living religious tradition. Remember the Navajo man who considered himself poor because he did not have a single song? His poverty was not because he was not familiar with any songs, but because he had no songs that he could assume the responsibility of performing as religious acts.[12]

It is impossible to recreate in writing the experience of a Navajo in the context of the performance of any prayer, for it is an act that engages all of the senses and a lifetime of personal experience in the culture. But even a brief description of the prayer performance adds much to an understanding of the cultural and religious processes engaged as well as a sense of the experiential dimensions evoked by the performance.

The particular prayer quoted is performed as part of a healing ceremonial known as Flintway, which focuses on healing internal injuries or those involving a loss of consciousness or vitality. The complex ceremonial may last a number of days and nights and includes many different ritual processes. It occurs in a Navajo hogan that is sanctified by a ritual blessing. This rite identifies the house with the creation hogan built at the place where the Navajo deities emerged on the earth surface. This blessing establishes the house as a microcosm. The part of the ceremonial in which the prayer is performed involves the ritual bathing of the individual who is being treated, the tying of a flint or jewel onto a medicine pouch, and the recitation of the prayer in a litany fashion by the one being treated and the "singer" or official responsible for performance of the entire ceremonial and the knowledge of its ways. The correspondence of ritual and speech acts contributes to the significance of the performance.

Furthermore, this whole ritual process exists in the context described in Navajo stories. The origin of Flintway is recounted in the story of the healing of the hunter by Gila Monster, outlined in chapter 2. This story is well known to the Navajo people, and, in some sense, it is dramatically brought before them in the ceremonial performance of Flintway. The Flintway ceremonial is performed in the cultural context described in the stories of emergence and creation. That context is evoked with the blessing of the ceremonial hogan in the very first ritual act.

In the performance of the Flintway ritual bath, songs are sung that refer to Gila Monster and to the powers of his medicine bundle. Songs are sung that identify the bath with the preparation for creation of the world in the beginning. The performance of the ritual bath purifies and places the one being treated in the environment of the cosmic forces of creation.

During the prayer, the person being treated ties a flint, a bead, or a jewel onto a medicine pouch as an offering. This is the sacrifice or offering referred to in the prayer. The pouch is identified with the source of the powers that restored the lives of Gila Monster and the hunter in the story. In that story, it was Gila Monster's medicine pouches that performed the restoration. They were described as two human-shaped agates that restored life by stepping over the reassembled body of Gila Monster. When Gila Monster initiated the hunter youth into the knowledge of Flintway, he prepared a representation of his agates for use by Navajos. This was the origin of the Flintway cranebill pouches. The construction of these pouches is significant. They are made by removing the flesh and organs from the bodies of a male and female crane and drying their flesh and organs in the sun. The dried parts from the cranes are then replaced in the bills in their natural order. Within the skin of the crane that is left attached to the bill are placed large hollow reeds used as medicine containers. All of the medicines are ritually prepared. One pouch is identified as male, the other female. Only one is used, corresponding to the gender of the person being treated by Flintway.

Even the construction of the crane medicine pouches is a replication of Flintway. The cranes are disassembled and then reassembled in their proper order. They have many other associations with Flintway through the complex preparation of the medicines they contain.

Nor is it without significance that the crane is chosen as a central religious figure of Flintway. In the songs of Flintway, the crane is of interest to the Navajo in this context because of its migratory habits. It is a bird who always knows where to find the best conditions for life. It is a good parent because it always takes its young to a life-giving place. Navajos shout when they see the crane return, for it marks the return to Navajoland of good weather and life-giving conditions. For purposes of Flintway, through all of these associations the crane represents the power of restoration or return of life.

These few observations outline only the most dominant features of a rich, complex network of associations. But, remembering that many additional levels exist, a fuller appreciation of the prayer is possible. It is intoned in a litany fashion by the singer and the person being treated, that is, the singer intones a phrase, and the other person repeats it. The sound of Navajo people praying is distinct, in itself evoking many potent images to anyone familiar with it, especially to Navajos. The person being treated holds the appropriate cranebill pouch while praying and sits on the floor of the hogan, legs extended, facing east.

Flintway prayers are usually performed in sets, that is, the prayer quoted earlier is intoned a number of times with only minor changes in the wording from one recitation to the next. Each set addresses one of two types of figures in the initial line. One set addresses any of a group of deities associated with the waxing and waning of life, seasonal cycles, or diurnal rhythms. This group includes such figures as the Thunders, Cranes, and Sun Carrier. Flintway prayers may also address a second type of figure, entities associated with the cause of the injury or illness being treated. If one is injured in a fall, for example, the Earth, as an entity, may be addressed. Other changes in the wording of the prayer maintain correspondences with the figures being addressed for specific applications of the prayer.

In the first recitation of the prayer, an offering is attached to the pouch at the mention of sacrifice in the prayer. The description that follows of the journey of the figure addressed in the prayer refers to the incident in the Flintway story when the proper help must be found and brought to the person in need, recalling the efforts of the family of the hunter youth to acquire the help of Gila Monster. At another level, this part of the prayer recalls the life-giving associations with the return of the crane or the thunder. The journey itself as described is associated with the return of life.

In the next passage of the prayer, the cure is effected by a process of identifying and associating the one praying with the crane. By being identified with the crane, Navajos believe one obtains the life-giving attributes associated with the crane. The identification process is extended to full body by naming the feet, legs, body, mind, and voice, which in Navajo thought are the vital centers of the body and must be invoked to realize wholeness as well as holiness.

The conditions of restoration associated with orderliness, wholeness, and mobility are described in the prayer. The changes in verb tense through the prayer, future becoming present, consist of a series that draws attention to the effectiveness of the prayer performance. In this way it is shown that the effects sought by the prayer are accomplished in the very act of performing it.

Consider the power and meaning of the prayer performance. It is not difficult to understand how the prayer performance engages a Navajo person and to appreciate the creative and healing powers of the prayer. Note that the verbal meaning of the prayer is obvious. For all involved, the prayer bears little news. They know that restoration is desirable and that religious help is needed. The performance of the prayer, however, is a complex religious act that engages all the senses in response to its smells, sights, tastes, sounds, colors, and temperatures. It evokes meaningful images based on personal and cultural history. Much of the power proceeds from the network of interrelated images associated with the stories of Flintway and the creation of the Navajo world and to the invoked associations with aspects of the natural world like cranes and thunder.

In the cultural ritual performance of the prayer, the set of images may be carefully channeled to address the specific needs of the motivating situation. The effort is to identify the specific situation with cosmic processes and primordial events. In Flintway, one not only learns that he or she suffers with a heroic figure, but that it is also in the nature of life for one to be subject to such sufferings. There are occasions in its very process that life appears to wane. That is the lesson of the crane, of the sun, and of thunder.

CONCLUSION

When Knud Rasmussen was studying the Eskimo in the 1920s, he had an interesting experience. In collecting information on various aspects of Eskimo life among the Iglulik people in the Baffin Bay area he recorded statements about the rules of life, customs, and taboos. But he noted that whenever he asked them why they did or did not do these things, they did not answer him. Nonetheless, Rasmussen continued to ask for justifications. Finally Aua, chief spokesman for the people, took Rasmussen outside where the bitter wind was harshly blowing the snow. He pointed across the frozen landscape and said to Rasmussen,

> In order to hunt well and live happily, man must have calm weather. Why this constant succession of blizzards and all this needless hardship for men seeking food for themselves and those they care for? Why? Why?

Receiving no answer from Rasmussen, he took him to a nearby home. They entered, and Aua pointed out two shivering children huddled beneath skin rugs. Again Aua addressed Rasmussen,

> Why should it be cold and comfortless in here? Kuglo has been out hunting all day, and if he had got a seal, as he deserved, his wife would now be sitting laughing beside her lamp, letting it burn full, without fear of having no blubber left for tomorrow. The place would be warm and bright and cheerful, the children would come out from under their rugs and enjoy life. Why should it not be so? Why?

Again Rasmussen could not answer, and Aua led him to yet another home. This was the home of his sister Natseq, who was very ill. To Rasmussen he said,

> Why must people be ill and suffer pain? We are all afraid of illness. Here is this old sister of mine; as far as anyone can see, she has done no evil. She has lived through a long life and given birth to healthy children, and now she must suffer before her days end. Why? Why?[13]

This exchange illustrates the fundamental issues raised in this chapter.

Many of the traits associated with exclusively oral cultures, such as personalization, immediacy, and concreteness, may also be found in traditions that contain written records and texts. The performance of culture is largely oral whether or not there is writing, and oral characteristics are certainly not absent from written communications. Aua's point, it seems, was that Eskimos are not peculiar in being unable to explain in simple statements the nature of existence or certain acts of culture. When confronted with the same questions he plied to the Eskimos, Rasmussen too was unable to answer Aua's questions about the nature of existence in the Eskimo environment and doubtless he would have been little more successful at answering such questions in his own Danish environment. Yet, when Rasmussen confronted the details of Eskimo culture, a culture alien to him, he could not resist asking questions like "Why? What does it mean? Why do you do this?" I suggest that such questions are the product of a removed perspective and correspond more closely with literacy, with understanding through interpreting writing, than for the immediacy of orality and the performed aspects of culture. For the exclusively oral cultures of Native Americans, such questions do not arise.

Differences in modes of thought correspond with the presence or absence of writing in a culture. While I would firmly hold that all humankind is equal in terms of mental capacity and faculties of reason, I would also hold that writing introduces possibilities for exercising certain modes of thought that are difficult, if not impossible, without it. Certain ways of scrutinizing discourse and language events are facilitated by writing. The semipermanency of writing permits and encourages more extensive criticism and analysis. It overcomes the impossibility of juxtaposing language events that occur at widely varying times and places. When writing is present, the capacity of memory and the mental processes of recall and data comparison are not constraints on thought and the possibilities of certain kinds of intellectual activities are expanded. Certain cultural processes can also occur as a consequence. Based on the analysis and criticism of texts, one person may write his or her understanding of certain aspects of these documents. These writings, along with the texts on which they are based, can be scrutinized and written about by another person, and so on, thus forming a second order tradition of criticism and a type of intellection impossible without writing. This achievement comes at a price, of course, for writing is often only an abstraction or interpretation of a performed cultural event. Writing may also create a distance between a person and his or her verbal acts. The point is that approaching exclusively oral cultures, or even the performed aspect of any culture, from the perspective nurtured by writing may well result in forced conclusions and misunderstanding.

Returning now to the Eskimo example, Rasmussen's questions arose out of his own cultural past, the post-Enlightenment tradition of thought characterized in part by the collection, comparison, analysis, and criticism of data from a variety of cultures, an effort that greatly expands the range of human communication and knowledge. But the existence of this kind of enterprise depends on literacy. Questions of meaning and justification are the stock in trade of this kind of intellectual tradition for they are necessary in bridging the radical differences in surface appearance.

These differences in modes of thought have nothing to do with mental capacity or with stages in human or mental development. Rather, they are related to differences in modes of communication, to the presence or absence of writing.[14]

Approaching an understanding of Native American religions from a Western academic tradition based in literacy, it is necessary to be sensitive to the significance of these differences for they underlie certain distinctive aspects of Native American religions as well as some of the difficulties that must be overcome in order to gain an understanding of these religions. Where European-American academic thought tends toward analysis and criticism—that is, the breaking down of our subjects of interest and seeking principles that hold the pieces together—Native Americans tend toward synthesis and reflection—that is, they attempt to place the object of interest into a broader, often cosmic context—and they note the compatibility that gives expression to the significance of the object. An illness becomes bearable and curable if it is seen as part of the processes that are distinctive to the culture. A life is meaningful if its sufferings and joys, defeats and victories, degradations and elevations can be imagined as part of the human story. This process is inseparable from what I call religion.

NOTES

1. As reported from the work on the Omaha by Alice Fletcher in *American Indian Prose and Poetry,* ed. Margot Astrov (New York: John Day, 1946), pp. 51–52.

2. Franz Boas, "Keresan Texts," *Publications of the American Ethnological Society* 8 (1928): 221, 224.

3. Account based on C. Hart Merriam, *An-nik-a-del: The History of the Universe* (Boston: Stratford, 1928), pp. 1–6.

4. See Leland C. Wyman, *Blessingway* (Tucson: University of Arizona Press, 1970), pp. 28–30; and Sam D. Gill, *Songs of Life* (Leiden: E. J. Brill, 1979), p. 6.

5. Knud Rasmussen, *The Netsilik Eskimos—Social Life and Spiritual Cultures,* Report of the Fifth Thule Expedition, 1921–1924, vol. 8 (Copenhagen: Gyldendalske Boghandel, 1931), p. 15.

6. Ibid., pp. 16, 321.

7. Willard W. Hill, "The Agricultural and Hunting Methods of the Navajo Indians," *Yale University Publications in Anthropology* 18 (1938): 52.

8. Rasmussen, *The Netsilik Eskimos,* p. 321.

9. Dagmar Fruechen, ed., *Peter Freuchen's Book of the Eskimo* (New York: World, 1961), p. 283.

10. Rasmussen, *The Netsilik Eskimos,* pp. 11–12.

11. For a presentation and discussion of this tale, see Alan Dundes, *The Study of Folklore* (Englewood Cliffs, N.J.: Prentice-Hall, 1965), pp. 269–76. The text by Cushing was originally published in *Zuni Folk Tales* (New York: Knopf, 1901), pp. 411–22.

12. For a discussion of performance, see Dell H. Hymes, "Breakthrough into Performance," in *Folklore: Performance and Communication,* ed. Dan Ben-Amos and Kenneth S. Goldstein (The Hague: Mouton, 1975), pp. 11–74.

13. Knud Rasmussen, *The Intellectual Culture of the Caribou Eskimo,* Report of the Fifth Thule Expedition, 1921–1924, vol. 7 (Copenhagen: Gyldendalske Boghandel, 1930), pp. 54–56.

14. See Jack Goody, *The Domestication of the Savage Mind* (Cambridge: Cambridge University Press, 1977), especially pp. 36–44, 150.

4

❧

Action and Performance

On a cold, moonless February night, I walked the zigzag road up the mesa to the Hopi village of Shipaulovi. Most of the houses were dark. Light came only from the hatchways atop the several kivas of that tiny village. The yellow lantern light glowing from these partially subterranean ceremonial chambers gave away the places from which the sonorous songs softly permeated the crisp night air. As I arrived at the top of the mesa, a young Hopi man came from a dark house and asked my business. Finding that I had come to see the night dances, he accompanied me to the top of one of the kivas, where we peered through the hatchway to watch the kachinas dancing within. Several other blanket-wrapped young people joined us in the cold.

The line of awesomely beautiful masked figures sang to the drummed accompaniment and danced in a stately fashion around the perimeter inside the kiva. Small children, married adults, and elders lined the rectangular kiva on wooden benches. From the middle of the floor beneath the ladder that led into the kiva a stove spread warmth throughout.

While we watched the dance, a second group of kachinas approached from below the mesa edge, having finished their dance in a kiva there. Some removed their masks and chatted quietly as they waited for the group of kachinas in the kiva to conclude their performance. One kachina who remained masked would occasionally approach the top of the kiva and utter a distinctive call to announce the presence of his group.

After we watched several of these performances, the Hopi youth I had joined suggested that we go to First Mesa some miles to the east, where other night dances were occurring. I agreed, and on this short midnight ride we talked of his family and his future. During our conversation, he turned to the subject of the night dances for a brief explanatory comment, perhaps because I had not asked about them. He said of them only, "What they are doing is mostly a dance for rain." I nodded my head, indicating that I understood what he meant, but I did not.

We arrived at First Mesa, where there was much activity. As the night progressed, more and more teenagers and young unmarried adults appeared, strolling about the villages. Blanket-wrapped, they gathered atop the kivas to watch the dances.

Each kiva in the village is represented by a group of kachinas who rotate from kiva to kiva to sing and dance throughout the night. The view from inside the kiva is remarkably different from that at the hatchway atop the kiva. From within, the night is a continual parade of beautiful, powerful deities who are invited into the microcosmic domain to sing and dance. From the kiva top, the view is rather like that of a play from the backstage wings. One sees the performance taking place, yet from an awkward vantage, and also sees the actors preparing their costumes and awaiting their cues to enter the performance stage. But from another perspective, this offstage area is the real world too, and the courting and social activities of the young people who occupy this space are clear evidence of it.

I have thought a lot about the explanation given by that young Hopi man, "They dance for rain," for I have heard it many times from other Hopi and other Native Americans. I believe that Hopis make such statements intending them in both the literal sense, that is, to dance causes rain to fall, and in the much broader figurative sense, that is, the connection of dancing and rain evokes the whole Hopi way of life—values, cultural and religious practice, art.

Though it seems unnecessary, there is a tendency to approach statements that may appear incredulous with a pejorative valuation based on seeming scientific savvy, as primitive, magic, or myth. That is, taken literally, to believe dancing causes rain is simply wrong and such statements are explained away with stock responses. A common alternative is to understand ritual, cultural, and aesthetic elements of cultures on the basis of a linguistic model. These complex events are easily seen as comprised of elements each of which clearly corresponds with something of significance. It is then a short step to think that these complexes comprise something like a language. The constituitive elements are considered symbols that are decodable in terms of their meanings, understood usually as that for which they represent. But this approach does not produce much more than a catalog of correspondences. These cultural complexes are doubtless full of meaning, yet they do not often yield, with any satisfaction, the equivalent of meaning in language. The translation of performances, events, enactments, and actions into some statement of meaning is invariably reductive to the point of the obvious or the irrelevant. Meaningful does not equate with meaning.

The tendency is to focus on what appears so obviously important, but with the result of completely ignoring, not even seeing, what, to Native Americans, is fundamental. Consider a wonderful illustration. Some years ago, a couple of folklorists were interested in the symbolism of the Hopi kachina sash. The sash is a wide, white, woven cotton cloth that is wrapped around the waist of the kachina dancer in such a way that the ends hang down on one side to the length of the dance kilt. On the ends of the sash are colorfully eye-catching embroidered designs. These folklorists pursued their study of the sash symbolism by discussing the significance of the embroidered designs with a number of Hopi. They found general agreement, with some variation correlating with village and mesa. With growing satisfaction that they were coming to understand how the Hopi regard the meaning of the sash, they were surprised when one Hopi told them that they had ignored what was to him the most important part of the sash—the sash itself. He explained that the designs mean little apart from their grounding on the sash, for only when they are on the sash can they be danced.

This suggests that the significance of Native American religious symbols is not something that can be determined by isolating and decoding particular symbols, that is, by finding out what they stand for. Rather, the fullness of these symbols is realized in the action of their performance. What at first appears as nothing but the background on which symbols are sewn turns out to be fundamentally significant from the perspective of the culture to which the symbols speak.

It is important to come to terms with the way to view and to understand the significance of religious actions and performances. Otherwise there is little hope to understand much about the aspects of culture that bear evidence of Native American religions. Native Americans rarely express their religious beliefs in terms of creeds, religious dogmas, or theologies, but rather in the performative forms of dance, ritual movement, and the use of religious objects. These actions engage the individual at every passage in the life cycle, and they engage the community in every significant activity that constitutes the community way of life. Native American religions are inseparable from their enactment.

RELIGIOUS PAINTINGS

Native American religious artifacts and painted surfaces and objects are usually considered by outside observers as works of art. They have been extensively collected and displayed in museums and art galleries. Where collection is impossible because of the nature of the artifact, they are reproduced in one manner or another for display. Consequently, the principal view of religious objects has been from an aesthetic perspective, not a religious one. Viewing from this perspective usually strips the items from their grounding in culture, removing them from the whole milieu of religious beliefs and practices. The background on which the designs are embroidered is not seen. The designs cannot dance.

Sometimes shock or surprise has been expressed with regard to the treatment Native Americans give their own creations. Some have wondered why the beautiful and very elaborate murals painted on Pueblo kiva walls were whitewashed and painted over again and again. Some have wondered why sandpainting, the creation of designs in colored sands, is such a temporary art form, for the paintings are destroyed shortly after their completion. From a perspective in which salability or monetary value is a measure of the aesthetic value, these paintings confound, they defy the system by which they seem to be valuable. This transiency is often circumvented on behalf of an artistic perspective by making reproductions that can be permanently displayed and sold. But what about the significance of the religious acts, which these creations are a vital part of? Navajo sandpainting is an important example.

In Navajo culture, sandpainting is a ritual procedure that forms a part of some religious ceremonials performed to cure an ailing person. Constructed on the floor of a ceremonial hogan, sandpaintings depict mythic persons and *diyin dine'é* (holy people), who in the associated stories have a connection with the cause and cure of the illness being treated. These figures must be carefully and accurately created from the memory of the singer or medicine man. No visual record is kept by the Navajo people, but hundreds of different patterns are known to exist. The finished picture provides a physical form in which the spiritual beings may manifest their presence. When corn pollen is sprinkled on the painting by the singer and the one for whom the ceremonial is being performed, the *diyin dine'é,* or holy people, become present in the sandpainting. In a sandpainting rite, the ailing person walks onto and sits in the middle of the painting, where he or she is identified with each of the holy people present in it. This identification is physically accomplished by a transfer of sands on the medicine-moistened hands of the singer. The sands are taken from the feet, legs, body, and head of each of the sandpainted figures and pressed onto the corresponding body parts of the person sitting on the sandpainting. When this identification is complete, the sandpainting, badly defaced during the rite, is completely destroyed by the singer, who scratches through it with a feather-tipped wand. The mixed sands are then removed and returned to nature.

From the Navajo perspective, each pattern painted in sand is appropriate to only certain of the many Navajo ceremonial ways. Each has its own story of origin, which in turn is framed by the whole Navajo ideology of creation. No sandpainting can be adequately understood without placing it in these contexts. Also, every ritual performance is distinctively appropriate to the specific cultural circumstances, the felt human needs, that call for it and are often considered in the selection of which sandpaintings will be used. In this way, certain features of a given sandpainting can be emphasized.

The meaning of any specific sandpainting for the Navajo is not discerned by analyzing the distinct symbols within the sandpainting, but rather by how the sandpainting evokes, interrelates with, and enacts the Navajo tradition. The richness of these designs emerges from the experience of hearing the stories, praying the prayers, living the way of life, suffering and being cured, all of which constitute Navajo tradition. To appreciate the significance and power of even one sandpainting requires that it be placed within these several levels of its cultural and religious contexts.[1] While that depth of consideration is more ambitious than can be presented here, certain statements can be made about the general religious character of Navajo sandpainting.

During the ceremonials in which sandpainting rites play a major role, the cause of the illness being treated is attributed to impaired relationships with specific life-giving forces. These forces are associated with certain holy people whose powers are directed against the life forces of the ailing person. In the ceremonial cure, rites are enacted to persuade the holy people to remove their life-threatening influence. But this in itself does not constitute a cure, for the person must be placed again in a state of order articulated in terms of place and relationship modeled on the creation of the Navajo world. The sandpainting rite is therefore also a rite of re-creation, in which the person is remade in a way appropriate to the conditions of the ailment. In this rite of re-creation, the sandpainting is the essential vehicle.

The person being recreated sits in the center of the sandpainting facing east, toward the opening in the circle that surrounds the sandpainting and toward the door of the hogan, facing in the direction of the road of life. This perspective on the painting cannot be shared by anyone. It is a view of the sandpainting from within it, being surrounded by it. Only portions of the sandpainting may be seen at any one time and these only from the center outward. To sit on the sandpainting and to be identified with the many holy people and cosmic dimensions that are alive in it is to experience the complexity and diversity, the dynamics and the tensions of the Navajo world, as presented in the surrounding painting. It is also to experience the one point common to all and therefore to see and to feel the unity and wholeness of the universe despite its diversity and tensions.

Placed in the religious context of rite and story, an illness suffered is an experience of the world at odds with itself, an incident within the drama of the Navajo world. The illness is overcome when the person realizes that, in some significant places, these tensions and oppositions can be balanced, can be brought into order, a synonym for health.

The beauty of a sandpainting is religiously important in presenting the fresh state of creation that is the very definition of beauty and health. But also of religious importance is the use to which sandpaintings are put, the healing of suffering individuals. From this perspective it is now possible to better understand why the paintings are destroyed after such use. They are not created as objects of art at all. They are the means by which re-creation, health, and beauty in life and the world are achieved. The sufferer finds his or her way to health from within the sandpainting, and in becoming a part of it, it disappears and becomes a part of him or her. The picture disappears in the process of a person coming to know the fullness and unity of the reality it represents. The destruction of the picture corresponds to the dissolution of the tensions and imbalances that gave rise to the suffering.

Navajo sandpaintings are often reproduced in books and articles. Knowing generally how they are viewed and used by Navajos, representations of sand-paintings drawn or painted on paper or canvas obscures the religious signifi-cance and emphasizes the aesthetic value. Navajos strictly forbid making rep-resentations of sandpaintings, and they are never kept as aesthetic objects. Even the use of sandpainting figures in the sand-glue craft is not approved by most Navajo singers. Sandpaintings must be destroyed by sundown on the day they are made. To Navajos they are not primarily aesthetic objects, they are instruments of a ritual process aimed at practical concerns. In terms of visual perspective, reproduced sandpaintings are always viewed from a position that would be directly above them and at such a distance that the painting is immediately seen as a whole, with each side equidistant from the eye. This view is impossible for ritual sandpaintings. When a painting six feet or more in diameter is constructed on the floor of a hogan only fifteen or twenty feet in diameter, the perspective from the periphery is always at an acute angle to the surface. A sandpainting cannot be easily seen as a whole. The most impor-tant point of view is that of the person being cured, and this person sees the painting from the inside out because he or she sits in the middle of it. These differences are basic and cannot be dismissed. The Navajo view is inseparable from the religious significance that sandpainting has for them.

From a perspective nearer that of the Navajo, sandpaintings are not the intended products of the creative process by which they are constructed. The product is a healthy human being or the re-creation of a well-ordered world. The sandpainting is but an instrument toward this creative act, and perhaps it is the wisdom of the Navajo to insist that it be destroyed in its use so that the obvious aesthetic value of the instrument does not supplant the human and religious concern that it serves.

To recall the hint from the Hopi about the meaning of the kachinas sash, it is not the constituitive elements in isolation, or the whole pattern so much, that are significant. It is rather what is done with them. It is the action they perform. The significance of much Native American symbolism is inseparable from the environment in which the symbols gain life and are put into action. Pueblo kiva murals depicted the appropriate background or context in which certain religious performances and actions could take place. They evoked the appropriate moods and atmosphere to frame the important, meaningful aspects of religious activities. As the seasons change, the concerns of religion change, and so must the background.

SELF-DIRECTED DESIGNS AND OBJECTS

In a study of the artifacts of Native Americans in the region east of the Rocky Mountains, it was found that the designs on these objects were often self-directed. For example, the designs on the toes of moccasins are oriented to the view of the wearer, not to others looking at the moccasins. This self-directed aspect was found in many objects like birchbark dishes, wooden bowls, drums, woven bags, snowshoes, breechcloths, and pipe bags. Craftsmen and users confirmed the intentionality of this orientation.[2]

Many museum collections of these objects contain no indication of the intended visual orientation of the objects. This has particular importance for any concern with religious significance in the case of effigy pipes. These are pipes with bowls carved in the shape of a figure—a bird, an animal, or a human being. Again, to understand the significance of the pipe from the perspective of the user, it must be removed from the glass museum case and placed in its religious context where its intended visual perspective can be appreciated. Among the Algonquin people, effigy pipes were used as aids in the concentration of thought. They were instruments of meditation. The pipe bowl bore the effigy of the guardian spirit or the familiar spirit of a shaman. These figures were carved on the bowl so that only when the smoker put the stem in his mouth did he come face-to-face with the representation of the spirit. Hence it was through smoking the pipe, drawing the tobacco smoke through the stem while concentrating on this effigy, that the smoker gained power from his guardian spirit.

Among the Sioux, effigy pipes sometimes took the form of a sitting human male, with the stem representing the penis. The Sioux also have self-directed effigy pipes depicting a bear facing the smoker. These were used by shamans whose power to cure and benefit war parties was centered on the spirit of the bear. In their ritual performances, these shamans personified bears, wearing fur costumes and moccasins with bear paws attached.

The religious meaning of the effigy pipe is inseparable from the act of smoking the pipe, from the relationships created through meditative smoking between the smoker and the spirit represented on the pipe. The fullness of meaning of pipes is inseparable from the spiritual relationship that occurred as a result of long hours of concentrated smoking of strong tobacco. The visual perspective was dictated by the use to which the pipe was intended. When not in use, the pipes were not displayed for aesthetic pleasure but carefully wrapped in their pipe bags.

ESOTERIC RELIGIOUS OBJECTS

Cultures over much of North America maintain medicine bundles. These bundles may be associated with a medicine pipe, as among the Northern Plains tribes; the calumet or friendship pipe, as in the Central Plains; or they may be simply a collection of powerful objects, as found in many parts of North America. Generally, these bundles are not public property and they are rarely, if ever, publicly displayed. A simple description of the objects in these bundles would scarcely hint that they are held to be highly important and powerful religious objects. The bundles commonly contain an array of items such as feathers, skins of birds and animals, bones (sometimes, as among the

Crow, even a human skull), teeth, herbs and other plants, pebbles, crystal rocks, hair, horse tails, deer tails, pigments, minerals, and many other objects of this kind. The simple, even commonplace appearance of the objects in a medicine bundle belies the religious importance of the bundle.

Bundles of various types have great powers that can be used in many ways for the benefit of the people. Bundles may have the power to cure, to invoke clairvoyance, to call game animals, to assure success in a hunt or war, even to attract a lover. Bundles are commonly considered to be alive and the place of residence of living spirits. They are kept by the most responsible persons and families and constantly cared for. Opening a bundle is ordinarily a complex affair, highly constrained by ritual proscription.

Students of bundles have found that the items included are often not standardized. Bundles used for essentially the same purpose, even within the same culture, may contain quite different items. Similar items in separate bundles may hold markedly different associations. This variety, not really so confusing, is itself a strong affirmation that these esoteric objects have potential for bearing much power and many values. It is through the stories of their origin, the histories of their owners and use, and the occasions and manner of their use that these objects come to bear significance of a magnitude that greatly surpasses their commonplace material character. It is in the power they generate, in the significance they evoke, in the awe and respect they command, that the powers of these medicine bundles must be understood and appreciated.[3]

MASKS

Masked performances take place on many Native American religious occasions. The very words mask and performance suggest that these ritual processes are somehow artificial, illusions, enactments of something else being imitated or represented. The word mask, in almost every sense of its meaning, indicates a covering, disguise, or concealment. Performance suggests the presentation of a dramatic work or an entertainment. Yet native people throughout North America hold that masks are living things, that in masked performances the deities themselves are present. It is in the conjunction, the interplay between the blatant falsity and artificiality of masks and the masker, that masking has the power to manifest the nonmaterial, the other.

Seneca False Faces

Distinctive among Native American masks are the Seneca False Faces. They are also found among other Iroquois people. They are worn by a society of men who perform at the new year's and green corn ceremonies in order to drive out the effects of witches and disease. They bring to presence the forces first shown by one of the twin brothers who created the world. According to the stories one brother created things to ease human life, while his brother kept pace creating nuisances, dangers, and death. When used in ritual, properly cared for masks make present the power of the nuisance-creating figure. They are also used throughout the year for purposes of curing illness.

The Seneca call these masks *gagosa,* which means simply face. The faces are carved into the trunk of a living basswood tree and removed, if possible, without killing the tree. The masks, which are painted all black or red or both black and red, usually have large eyes made of pieces of metal attached to the mask pierced in the center to form pupils. The often grotesquely distorted and exaggerated mouth and nose are distinctive features. The mouth often contains huge teeth or a hanging tongue. Each mask is topped with a long hank of hair.

These masks are carved by a member of the Society of Faces to present images revealed in a dream. In a man's dream the appearance of the face of his guardian spirit is revealed and he carves the mask to manifest that spirit. The carved faces are considered to be alive and are treated accordingly by their custodians. When not in use, they are hung facing the wall or are wrapped and carefully placed in a box or drawer. Periodically they are fed by smearing on their lips a thick gruel of parched cornmeal and maple sugar. They are also occasionally wiped with sunflower-seed oil "to keep their skin soft." Old masks shine with the patina of many applications of oil. Each mask is named and has its own personality. The masks are talked to, sung to, and addressed as grandfather. The faces are considered potent, for when properly used in ritual they manifest the powers of the Bad Twin who, when overcome by the Good Twin at the close of creation, was destined to aid in keeping the health and well-being of human beings.[4]

In this example, the face is not a mask at all, in the sense of being a covering or a disguise. Nor is it false in any sense. The wooden faces give physical presence to beings revealed through dreams. The wearing of the face is not to cover or disguise the wearer. It is to present and animate the real presence of the spirit.

Looking through the Mask: The Hopi Case

Among a number of Native American people, it is a common practice at rites of initiation into societies that use masks to present initiates with a view they have never had, the view from behind the masks, looking through the eyeholes. The uninitiated are carefully prevented from knowing about masks. They are never permitted to see masks that are not being worn or performers in ritual dress without their masks. When initiated, they are permitted for the first time to look through the eyeholes of the masks. It is tempting to understand this act as a method of educating the initiates to the unreality of the mask, that is, showing the uninitiated that, instead of a real being, the masked performer is actually only an impersonation. This understanding is not supportable. It is a matter of perspective. The perspective from which one gains the fullest experience of the mask is not that of looking *at* it at all, though this is certainly an essential stage in the process. The fuller appreciation is gained by looking *through* the eyeholes of the mask and seeing the effect it has on the world. That is why it is a privileged view of the initiated.

Don Talayesva, in his autobiography, tells of his participation in the Soyoko ritual, which is aimed at disciplining uninitiated children. In this ritual, monstrous-looking figures come to houses of misbehaving children and demand that the children be given to them as food to eat. In this ritual drama the parents bargain with the kachinas seemingly in order to save their children. The children's bad behavior costs the family considerably and this, along with the fear aroused by the kachinas, serves to encourage proper behavior. Talayesva describes a time when he wore the mask of the Giant Kachina and enacted this ritual process. He played his part well, with great effect on the children. That night Talayesva had a dream.

> I was tired and restless, and dreamed that I was still a Giant Kachina arguing for the children. I reached out my hand to grab a child and touched him. [Touching a child is considered inappropriate for fear of frightening a child to death.] The little one held up his hands to me, crying and begging to be set free. Filled with pity, I urged him to be a good child in order to free himself from the Giant Spirit. I awoke worried, with a lump in my throat, and bells ringing in my ears. Then I spat four times and decided that if I were ever the Giant again I would have a better-looking mask and speak in a softer voice.[5]

Looking through the mask from inside out, Talayesva experienced at once the power and force made present by his wearing the mask and his own human feelings about the masked being's effect on the world as reflected in the faces of the children.

Emory Sekaquaptewa spoke of his experience of performing as a Hopi kachina,

> I am certain that the use of the mask in the kachina ceremony has more than just an esthetic purpose. I feel that what happens to a man when he is a performer is that if he understands the essence of the kachina, when he dons the mask he loses his identity and actually becomes what he is representing. . . . The spiritual fulfillment of a man depends on how he is able to project himself into the spiritual world as he performs. He really doesn't perform for the third parties who form the audience. Rather the audience becomes his personal self. He tries to express to himself his own conceptions about the spiritual ideals that he sees in the kachina. He is able to do so behind the mask because he has lost his personal identity.[6]

Sekaquaptewa expresses the paradox of how one is at once enacting an impersonation but is also transformed into what he is impersonating. It is described in terms of perspective. One best sees the reality that oneself is manifesting by wearing the mask. While looking through its eyeholes, one gains a view from the vantage of the audience and is also able to know the reality the mask presents.

Kwakiutl Masks and the Notion of Place

Much has been written about the importance of the hierarchical social structure of Pacific Northwest Coast tribes and also about the fascinating array of masks used by these people. In order to understand the role of the mask, it is necessary to understand, in general terms, the Kwakiutl view of reality. It is identified with a grid of relationships defined in primordial times that is eternal. This grid of relationships identifies a fixed number of positions, to each of which belongs a name, referred to as a seat or standing place. Another way of designating the standing places that constitute reality is by crests, which in their highest form are masks. Indeed, the Kwakiutl word *keso* refers to both mask and crest. In Kwakiutl stories, the creation of the family lineages of human beings occurred when the ancestor to the lineage came down to earth, took off his animal mask, and became a human being.

The reality of names, crests, and masks is fixed and eternal. This reality is animated or given living form by the individual human beings who may temporarily bear the names and wear the masks. From this perspective, only those individuals who obtain a name and the privilege of wearing a mask at ceremonial performances enter into what is considered the true reality. Only those individuals have a claim to a fully meaningful role in life. For the Kwakiutl, the mask is what is real, and the wearer of the mask participates in that reality only by virtue of the privilege of wearing the mask.

Once again it is clear that the mask is not a covering or a disguise at all, but an appearance of that which, while seemingly artifice presents the real.[7]

As shown in these examples, masks are important not because they cover up or disguise. They are powerful because of what they make present: the spiritual reality, deities, or mythic characters. Masks cannot be translated or decoded because their meaningfulness is inseparable from what they make present—which, apart from the masks, could not be observed or expressed. It is the inexplicability of the human capacity even to grasp deep and spiritual levels of reality, much less to serve as its agent of manifestation, to which the masks gives full expression.

CLOWNS

Unfortunately outside observers have not been quick to recognize the important religious role of Native American clowns despite repeated testimony by Native Americans. Perhaps this was because early observers were so threatened and shocked by clown behavior, which is often not only crude and suggestive but may also be even sexually explicit and taboo, commonly seen amidst the most religious festivals and places, that they were incapable of seeing or believing what they were told.

Throughout much of the nineteenth and early twentieth centuries, Native American clowning was reported by outsiders in descriptions that scarcely hid the observers' disapproval of the actions they witnessed. Their use of Latin or English euphemisms to describe the explicit sexual and physical antics of the clowns doubtless reveals more about their own religious and cultural values than about the Native Americans they were observing. Yet clowning is an activity deeply important to many Native American religions. Native American clowns are many and varied. One possible way to discuss clowning is to consider several styles of behavior or methods they may use in their performances.

Being Contrary

A common approach taken by Native American clowns is that of being contrary, that is, doing everything the opposite of the way it is ordinarily done. Among the best known clowns who are masters of this style is the Sioux *heyoka* who rides backwards on his horse, puts his boots on the wrong feet, walks backward, wears heavy clothing in the summer and goes naked in the winter, says yes when he means no, and so on. The *heyoka* is not a deviant to be scoffed at and removed from society. Rather he is one who has received a vision of the Thunder Being, the personification of the principle that gives meaning and definition by countering the principle of normalcy and order. The *heyoka* is like the mask that makes the Thunder Being visible on earth. There is plenty that is humorous about the *heyoka* within his own society, but inseparable from the contrary behavior is the threat of disorder it poses, a threat like the destruction of the Thunder Being who brings storms and lightning. Yet the Sioux, when commenting about this aspect of *heyoka,* point to the creative results gained even from such threatening experiences. Thunder and lightning threaten destruction, but they accompany the refreshing rains of the storm. Likewise, while the contrary behavior of the clown threatens disorder, the values of normalcy are defined by contrast with the apparent absurdity of the clown behavior.

The Forbidden

A major role enacted by Native American clowns is the portrayal of all things that are forbidden, unnatural, or considered to be inhuman. Nineteenth-century observers were horrified by some of the actions of Pueblo clowns. They sometimes eat and drink dirt, excrement, urine, live mice, sticks, stones, and whatever is considered defiling. They appear nude and engage in explicit sexual activities, even in the most religious places during public performances. Just before 1900, Alexander Stephen, who was living among the Hopi, reported that a male clown dressed as a woman came into the plaza with a wash basin and began to wash "her" legs, spreading them to reveal beneath the

skirt a huge false vulva, a sight that brought much laughter from the specta-
tors. Another clown then appeared wearing a large false penis made from the
neck of a gourd. He approached the "female" clown and, expressing his sexual
attraction, engaged her in vigorous simulated copulation. All of this occurred
on a sacred shrine.

Examples of clowns engaging in ordinarily forbidden activities could be
multiplied. There is more than the powers of invoking opposites involved
here, and there is more than a demonstration of the interdependence of
destruction and creation. This action gains its power from the charge inseparable from pollution and dirt. Mary Douglas's *Purity and Danger* is enlightening
on this topic. Although she does not discuss Native Americans or clowns, she
helps us understand how Native Americans can describe these clown activities
as religiously important and as having such powers that they may cure people
and help the community in pursuit of its way of life.

Douglas asks the question that has surely crossed the minds of many
observers of these defiling clowns "Can there be any people who confound
sacredness with uncleanness?" She concludes that such a confusion is utterly
senseless and therefore turns to an exploration of the symbolism of dirt and
pollution, the symbolism engaged when the clowns perform acts which, from
any other point of view, would be considered almost unspeakable. She
reminds us that dirt (and subsequently forbidden actions) is created as a by-
product of the creation of order. There is an initial state of nondifferentiation,
that is, when nothing was distinguishable from anything else. The process of
creation, which requires differentiation, results in meaningful order, but dirt, as
a product of the same creative process, constantly threatens the distinctions
being made. Dirt is like the category weed, it is a thing out of place, a petunia
in an onion patch. For a thing to be recognized as dirt, one must have a clear
notion of the character of order, the requirements of proper place, and the
compelling significance of that created order. Even beyond that, dirt or pollution has the ability to evoke, albeit often by revulsion, an experience of the
powers that bring order into the world. The highly evocative powers of a polluting act bring one into touch with that which is fundamental to creation,
that which gives compelling significance to a created order. Dirt, like formless-
ness, invokes the beginning stages of creation and growth as much as decay.
And that is its significance.

To engage in the defiling acts of this type of clowning is not simply to
manifest the counterforces that, when balanced, make the universe cohere, as
do the contrary clowns, it is to present the experience of chaos, of no order at
all, of nondifferentiation. The danger risked in these activities is accompanied
by the acquisition of power—for in transgressing such ominous boundaries,
the clowns engender the forces of differentiation that distinguish order from
chaos and thereby create a meaningful world. There is a deep paradox here,
and its inexplicability is precisely what these clowns master and invoke. Defiling clowns are often considered even more powerful than the medicine people or shamans.[8] Importantly, these defiling acts of clowns could never be
done apart from the appropriate ritual framework. Only in this controlled

framework can the engendered powers be used for a creative purpose. Such acts performed out of the bounds of religious structures would be considered destructive and not tolerated.

The Portrayal of Human Folly

Native Americans reflect on and express insight into the character of human beings through clowning that portrays human folly. Social commentary and control are also exacted by ritual clowns. This type of clowning is usually an exaggeration of the needs and drives distinctive of being human. These acts are not contrary to the ordinary, nor are they a defilement or pollution. They are simply an exaggeration, like a cartoon. Clowns are well known for being gluttonous, willing to do anything for something to eat. Clowns also portray failure to see the obvious and play the fool as a result. They learn slowly after making the same mistakes over and over again. They are greedy to the point of destroying what they desire in an unwillingness to share. Their sexual needs are expansive and insatiable and not at all disguised. Clowns often approach people in the audience with sexual gestures and engage in all sorts of sexual innuendos. They enact skits portraying aspects of human sexuality. Such clowns often strike a marked contrast to the concurrent appearances of the masked deities. The clown performances often present an image of the difficulties that human beings encounter, as a result of their nature, in their attempts to attain human fulfillment.

When Humor Turns to Fear

In all clown performances, the distance between the clowns and the audience is a key to the effect they achieve. Even for outsiders, clown antics are outrageously funny so long as they can be observed at a comfortable distance. To see clowns engage in sexual activities with one another or approach an observer in a mocking or threatening manner is very funny. I once saw a group of Hopi clowns approach an Anglo observer sitting on a chair in the dance plaza. These seats are unspokenly reserved for the older women. Four clowns grabbed him, one each on his arms and legs. They lifted him high in the air again and again, finally leaving him lying on his back on the ground with his arms and legs flapping like an overturned bug. But such a funny sight as this can turn to fear if one happens to be the object of such activity or is drawn by the clowns into unwilling participation.

In the matter of this delicate dividing line between humor and fear, clowns are also masters. To be only threatening would greatly limit the impact of clowning, eliminating all the subtleties of their humor. Yet to eliminate the element of fear altogether would weaken their power, reducing them to mere entertainers. Crossing that line from humor to threat evokes deep emotions and manifests the powers that shape and could also destroy the world.

RITUAL MATERIALS IN ACTION

As with the clowns, much attention has been given to Native American sacrificial rites like the widespread sun dance, in which many individuals shed blood as part of the ceremony, and the Skidi Pawnee sacrifice of a captive girl to Morning Star.

The Skidi Pawnee sacrifice apparently occurred only when Mars was a morning star. The rite originated in a dream in which Morning Star appeared to a Skidi man and directed him to capture a sacrificial victim. This man would capture a girl from an enemy village and return her to the chief of the Morning Star village where she was well treated until her sacrifice. Four days of ritual concluded the morning of the fifth day with the bloody sacrifice of the girl.

Morning Star was commemorated with a ritual bundle that held many ceremonial objects used on this occasion. During the first three days, songs were sung describing the exploits of Morning Star. Tobacco smoke and dried meat were offered to the Morning Star bundle. The girl was purified with smoke, painted red, and dressed in a black costume. Her captor, who personified the Morning Star, was also dressed in a ritual costume. Cosmic symbolism appears throughout the ceremonies. On the last evening, the priests sang a song describing the journey of the Morning Star in search of the Evening Star, while one of the priests danced with his war club about the lodge obliterating the four circles inscribed on the floor to represent the four world quarters. A series of songs of Evening Star were then sung during which counting or tally sticks from the bundle were laid down marking the progression of the victim from the human world to the divine world of celestial beings.

Then priests painted the girl's body, black on one half and red on the other, and they set out for the place of the sacrifice. In that place a scaffold consisting of two uprights and five crosspieces had been erected, each part corresponding with the world structure. The girl was lifted onto the scaffold and tied into position so that as the morning star arose, her captor, personifying Morning Star, approached her. With a bow and arrow, he shot her through the heart while another man struck her on the head with a war club. The officiating priest immediately opened her breast with a flint knife and smeared his face with her blood, while her captor caught the falling blood on dried buffalo meat and corn seeds. Finally, all male members of the tribe approached her and shot arrows into her body.

One priest remained after the others had dispersed to take down the body and lay it on the ground, head to the east. The blood-soaked buffalo meat and corn were burned under the scaffold as an offering. Finally, the priest sang songs describing how the body, eaten by various animals, would return to the earth.[9]

In this sacrificial rite, reminiscent of the bloody sacrifices of the Aztec in Mexico, ritual items and actions were used to reenact the history of the people who find their identity and source of life bound with the Morning Star bundle.

But no material here is so potent as that of blood. Blood is not a substance that can be kept in a bundle or used passively. Blood, in ritual use, is active and can be nothing else. To shed blood in sacrifice can not be a passive or simply a representative act. The bloody sacrificial rites once performed by the Skidi Pawnee powerfully express the inexplicable interdependence of life and death, a relationship symbolized by the rising and setting of the red planet Mars, the chase of the Morning Star by the Evening Star, where the death of one signals the birth of the other, the life and death of the sacrificial victim, the living of humans by the dying of animals, a similar interdependence of humans and plants as suggested by the inclusion of corn, the consumption of the victim's body by animals, and the blood that signifies the substance of vitality as well as death. Blood as a substance invokes great power when it is brought into action by rites of sacrifice. Then it becomes so potent as to be central to the commemoration of the religious history of a people and to give expression to the most profound and inexplicable principles of life.

The power of blood is shaped by the cultural and ritual context in which it appears. For example, the values associated with the blood of menstruation outside a cultural context is ambiguous. In some cultural contexts, it is the most polluting and threatening of substances. The menstruant is isolated from others, especially potent men, a practice common among Algonquin people. But the blood of menstruation can just as well symbolize the powers of fecundity. In this case, the menstruant is in possession of powerful medicine and contact with her is sought by the ailing that they might be cured, by children that they might grow and learn, and by the aged that they might continue to live. This attitude is common in the American Southwest.

Many substances and materials have widespread use as religious symbols in native North America. Like blood, they are often associated with life and capable of mediation between categories that are clearly distinct but mutually interdependent. Perhaps no substance, for example, is so widely used for its religious significance as tobacco. It is associated with food, with the breath, with the lungs and heart. In the act of smoking, the tobacco enters into the vital processes of human beings by being taken into the lungs and is then exhaled to rise to the sky and dissipate. It is often associated with acts of prayer and mediation between the human and other-than-human worlds.

Pollens of corn and other plants are widely used as religious symbols, especially among agricultural people. Pollen is the substance that moves between male and female plants to produce fertilization. As such, it is inseparable from life and fertility. Its capacity and function as a mediator constantly associates it, like tobacco, with prayer and communion. Pollen is strewn or eaten in gestures of blessing.

Native American ritual acts and ritual dress often involve the extensive use of feathers. Among many people, nothing is more potent and meaningful than feathers. Feathers can scarcely be symbolic apart from images of motion, flight, air, and the sky. The types of birds from which feathers can be collected and the habits and character of those birds provide an endless potential for religious symbols.

CONCLUSION

Let me end this chapter by recalling the statement I was told by a Hopi man in explanation of the Hopi dances, "They dance mostly for rain." The significance of the statement and the ritual dances to which it is referred cannot be expressed in terms of a message. Their significance must be seen in terms of the religious processes of which they are a part. The dances are deeply rooted in the traditions of the people, their history, their stories and poetry, their whole way of life. This is also true for a wide range of Native American religious actions and performances. Religious performances do not simply comment on life or commemorate things past or entertain, yet they do all of these to some extent. They set off a process by which life and a way of life for a specific people gains its value and identity. While one cannot adequately simply decode the message of religious actions, they serve to make life itself significant, and they do so by their ability to grasp, to express, and to engender the transcendent as well as the paradoxical and inexplicable. If religious actions and performances could be completely and efficiently translated or explained they would be unnecessary. Precisely because this cannot be done, religious rites, actions, and performances are significant and create significance. They evoke the fundamental structures and patterns from the tradition and thereby establish meaningful religious and cultural forms in which the future may unfold.

In terms of the Hopi perspective, dancing is the religious and social process through which the structures and patterns of Hopi culture are defined and expressed. Through the movement of dancing, culture and its underlying religious principles are brought into being and enacted. Dancing then is nothing short of giving life, an act so appropriately represented in the desert regions of northeastern Arizona by the essential rain.

NOTES

1. I have in this way discussed the Whirling Logs sandpainting; see Sam D. Gill, "Whirling Logs and Coloured Sands," in *Native Religious Traditions,* ed. Earle H. Waugh and K. Dad Prithipaul (Waterloo, Ontario: Wilfrid Laurier University Press, 1979), pp. 151–63.

2. See Ted J. Brasser, *"Bo'jou, Neejee!" Profiles of Canadian Indian Art* (Ottawa: National Museum of Man, 1976).

3. For sources on bundles, see Ake Hultkrantz, *Prairie and Plains Indians* (Leiden: E. J. Brill, 1973), pp. 21–25;

George Dorsey, *Traditions of the Skidi Pawnee* (New York: Houghton Mifflin, 1904), pp. 1–14, 55–57; and Clark Wissler, *Ceremonial Bundles of the Blackfoot Indians,* Anthropological Papers, vol. 7, part 2 (New York: American Museum of Natural History, 1912).

4. Anthony F. C. Wallace, *The Death and Rebirth of the Seneca* (New York: Vintage, 1969), pp. 79–93.

5. Don Talayesva, *Sun Chief: The Autobiography of a Hopi Indian* (New Haven: Yale University Press, 1942), p. 184.

6. Emory Sekaquaptewa, "Hopi Indian Ceremonies," in *Seeing With A Native Eye,* ed. Walter H. Capps (New York: Harper and Row, 1976), p. 39.

7. See Irving Goldman, *The Mouth of Heaven: An Introduction to Kwakiutl Religious Thought* (New York: John Wiley, 1975), pp. 62–63, 228.

8. For a discussion of pollution and taboo, see Mary Douglas, *Purity and Danger: An Analysis of Concepts of Pollution and Taboo* (Baltimore: Penguin, 1966), especially pp. 188–210.

9. See G. A. Dorsey, "The Skidi Rite of Human Sacrifice," *Proceedings of the International Congress of Americanists* 15 (1907): 65–70; and Ralph Linton, "The Origin of the Skidi Pawnee Sacrifice to the Morning Star," *American Anthropologist* 28 (1926): 457–66.

5

Roads of Life

For most Native Americans, life unfolds in the midst of a landscape endowed with the symbolic significance that provides orientation and direction. The mountains, the cardinal directions, the celestial bodies, and many other natural features commonly reflect complex religious values. The cycle of human life, the journey from birth to death, is brought into line with cosmology by being depicted as a process of movement within the landscape. Life is a road one travels, and the proper course for that road is often replicated in many cultural objects.

The road of life is often described as an orientation. The Hopi, for example, consider the lifeway as oriented as from west to east. This is the direction in which the rain clouds, identified with kachinas and dead ancestors, move to bring the life-giving rain. This is the direction in which the Hopi ancestors traveled when they migrated to their present homelands from the place of their primordial emergence into this world. It is the direction one faces to greet the sun when it arises from its night home. The Hopi believe that an unwell person must reorient his or her mind to an easterly direction. The ill are accused of thinking in a westerly orientation.

The road of life is graphically depicted as a labyrinth by the Pima and Papago of the southern Arizona deserts. This symbolic design is often woven as a pattern in baskets. It consists of a circle, in the center of which a small circle represents the earth. Beginning in the center, four lines radiate in each direction in the pattern of a single path labyrinth. The directional lines are associated with the four winds who are messengers of the culture hero and creator deity *I'i'toi,* represented in humanlike form at the entrance to the maze. The labyrinth depicting the road of life thus portrays the difficulties of life, its conflicts, and its confusions, but it goes beyond this. The symbol of the labyrinth shows that life is directed toward the center and that one who follows the path under the direction of *I'i'toi* will find the goal in the center despite the unavoidable complexities and sorrows in life.

Peyote religion, the Native American Church, has become a widespread religion among Native Americans. The rituals of Native American Church meetings depict the road of life according to the peyote way as a line drawn on a crescent-shaped altar. At the center of the road, in the middle of the altar, is placed a large, perfect peyote cactus button which represents Chief Peyote, the principal spirit or deity engaged in the peyote religion.

For the Oglala Sioux, the road of life is distinguished not only by its directional orientation, which is from north to south, but also by a red color designation. North is the direction associated with purity and south with the source of life. Thus, an orientation along this axis is the proper orientation for life. The red road is in opposition to the east-west orientation, which is described by the Sioux as the blue or black road. The follower of this path is thought to be distracted, ruled by his senses, and selfish.

The Delaware/Lenape depict the road of life in their Big House ceremonies and the Navajo depict it in their common symbolic pattern of the open circle.

Native Americans do not isolate a category of culture or human activity that they specifically call religion. Few words exist in Native American languages that translate closely to the word religion. Religion permeates all aspects and domains of Native American life and culture. Native Americans explicitly distinguish many ritual and ceremonial occasions. These often correspond with momentous passages in the cycle of life. Considered together for any Native American culture, this sequence of rituals comprises an important segment of religion. These formal religious activities are often complex and serve a variety of functions. Through them, the individual gains knowledge of tradition, access to the privileges of performing certain vital roles in culture, and access to the powers for the meaningful navigation of the road of life.

Focus on the religious life of the individual in Native American cultures shows that life is lived as a journey along a road well charted and carefully directed by the religious tradition. Many elements in Native American religious traditions are engaged at each moment in the process of life from conception to death. This road may be seen as a nurturing ambience as well as a narrow and precarious path. Further, while this ambience guides and directs the actions of each person, making his or her life meaningful from the smallest to the grandest terms, it also provides the person with access to processes of individuation, that is, to the way in which an individual is a creative, distinct human being situated within a community joined together by a common religious tradition.

Only a modest summary of any of these religious events is possible here, for the variety of data in North America is immense. Select examples may illustrate something of the many ways in which a religious tradition informs and activates the religious life of persons within the culture. These examples will be generally ordered to correspond with significant points or activities in the process of the life of an individual person. This approach should serve as an introduction to the various kinds of elements that may be present in any Native American religion, as well as a suggestion of how these elements function religiously and culturally.

BEGINNING THE JOURNEY

Human Origins

In the era of creation before human beings peopled the land of the Navajo, Changing Woman became the personification of the source and powers of life. The world was cleared of monsters through her benevolent and thoughtful acts and made ready for the origin of the Navajo people. When all was ready, Changing Woman took residence in a home especially prepared for her. It is located in the ocean beyond the western edge of the land. Her house has four rooms, each of which corresponds to a domain and season of the world. It is the nature of Changing Woman, as her name suggests, to change from youth to adolescence to adulthood and then to old age in a never–ending cycle. As she changes through the four stages of life, she takes residence in the room of her house that corresponds to her respective life stage. In her home, Changing Woman lives in correspondence with the earthly life cycles of the people to whom she gave origin.

In the creation era when the world had been put in place, Changing Woman began to think about what should be done. She thought of the creation of human beings. She went to the first of the four rooms of her house and there rubbed off the outer layer of skin from her chest. She mixed this with pollen and formed it into a ball, which she placed in a basket on the side corresponding with the room she occupied. Then she proceeded through the other rooms, rubbing balls of skin from her back, her right arm, and her left arm. She then covered the basket and stepped across it four times, whereupon from the basket arose four men and four women, the progenitors of the first four Navajo clans. She dressed the men in fabrics and the women in jewels. Then, to distinguish them as human, she gave them speech and instructed them to tell stories to each other. She continued to instruct them in all the ways of human beings. She told them of the *diyin dine'é,* holy people, and how they might be contacted. She told them of the appropriate duties and activities for men and for women. She told them of the special concerns to which each of the clans should direct their attention. She instructed them about their houses, their fields, their animals, and their water. At dawn the next day, she sent them on their way to the land she had prepared for them.

For the Navajo, the road of human life is thus coincident with the way of the entire world.

Many Native American people articulate the model for human life in stories of creation. Human life often corresponds with the ways of the world. As already seen in many ways, Native American religious traditions inform human beings of the meaning of the world in terms of correspondences between the ordinary and the cosmic, between the material and the spiritual. The division of sexes, the organization of clans, the entire social structure, and the life process of individuals all correspond and interweave.

The origin of human beings is not always a part of the stories of the origin of the world. Where it is included, it tells much about the concept and way of life and the notions of destiny held by the people of that tradition. Many Native American hunting people, for example, trace the origin of human beings to animals or from the progeny of an animal–human marriage. More common among cultivating people are stories that do not recount the creation of human beings but rather are concerned with how they came to the present world, a journey, an emergence. For a people to have their way of life established by deities or creators in the primal era assures the meaningfulness of life and the promise for its fulfillment. Such an origin also establishes life as a religious activity, for life is in accordance with the creators and with the processes of the world.

Conception and Birth

The sexual act of procreation and the period of pregnancy are not usually celebrated by ceremonials of any extent. Yet, the prenatal period is often seen as a period of intense regulation of the activities of the mother, in particular, but sometimes also of the father and other relatives. Food, social relationships, work, even events that the mother and father witness are often considered to have an effect on the health and destiny of the new life. It is common for people who suffer illness or strife, even when well into adulthood, to attribute it to incidents that occurred while they were carried in their mother's womb. In light of this attribution, it is notable that many Native American autobiographies begin with an account of the prenatal period and birth. In his autobiography *Sun Chief,* Don Talayesva, a Hopi, described the incident in which he was conceived as twins. Because the Hopi do not receive twin birth as a happy event, his pregnant mother underwent a rite in which the twins were joined together. In his words, they were "twisted into one."[1]

In some cultures ceremonies and prayers are given for the expectant mother as her time of delivery approaches to assure good health to her and her child.

Birth is an event carefully regulated by tradition, but rarely is it an event for ceremony. Public events are more likely to occur on the occasion when the infant and its mother are presented to the community and to the deities. A period of confinement is often required. Special prayers, such as the following one from Zuni, may be said to bless the newborn. On the eighth day of the infant's life, its head is washed by its father's female relatives and corn meal is placed in its hands. Then, at the moment of sunrise, it is taken out of doors and faced to the east. As the prayer is spoken by the paternal grandmother, corn meal is sprinkled toward the rising sun.

> Now this is the day.
> Our child,
> Into the daylight
> You will go out standing.
> Preparing for your day,
> We have passed our days.
> When all your days were at an end,
> When eight days were past,
> Our sun father
> Went in to sit down at his sacred place.
> And our night fathers
> Having come out standing to their sacred place,
> Passing a blessed night
> We came to day
> Now this day
> Our fathers,
> Dawn priests,
> Have come out standing to their sacred place.
> Our sun father
> Having come out standing to his sacred place,
> Our child,
> It is your day.
> This day,
> The flesh of the white corn,
> Prayer meal,
> To our sun father
> This prayer meal we offer.
> May your road be fulfilled
> Reaching to the road of your sun father,
> When your road is fulfilled
> In your thoughts (may we live)
> May we be the ones whom your thoughts will embrace,
> For this, on this day
> To our sun father.
> We offer prayer meal.
> To this end
> May you help us all to finish our roads.[2]

Other moments early in the life of an infant, such as the loss of the umbilical cord, the first laugh, and the occasion of naming are also commonly given special acknowledgment in North America in the form of ceremony and feast.

Naming

Native American views of names and the process of naming are illuminated by a phrase N. Scott Momaday attributed to his grandfather "a man's life proceeds from his name, in the way that a river proceeds from its source."[3] With identity tied so closely to name, the selection and bestowing of names are often matters of ceremony and complex customs. Among many cultures, a child's name is chosen to identify him or her with an admired elder or ancestor, or may even serve to reincarnate an ancestor. The name is sometimes identified with the soul and hence with the very force of life. Names are also identified with stations of reality, as in the Kwakiutl culture previously described. The Eskimo reveal a similar view, identifying a name with the reality to which it is attached in a practice that accompanies the birth. As the mother is about to deliver, an elderly woman is called in to pronounce as many eligible names as she can recall. The child comes forth from its mother when it hears its name being called.

Many Native American cultures do not consider an unnamed child to be fully alive or to be fully human. If a child dies before it is named where this belief prevails, funeral rites may either be greatly abbreviated or not done at all. It is believed that the life force will soon reenter the mother's womb to be born again.

The life road is not simply a series of distinct steps, each leading to the next. The life road is rather a way. As one proceeds along the road, he or she accumulates the knowledge of, and thus gains identification with, this way of living. For example, the act of naming has major significance because it is much more than a once-used custom by which a person gains a label. In many Native American cultures, naming is a practice engaged at many points throughout life. One may receive names as awards for acquiring prestige. A name may be given a young man after returning from his first successful hunt or war party or after completing initiation into a particular society or order. The Choctaw referred to all boys, until they earn a name, by a name that would translate literally as "Choctaw without a name."

Nicknames are often used to identify distinctive personal features or characteristics, but they may also be used to ridicule or criticize the actions of any person. Pronouns are commonly very complex in native languages. Their use may require that one precisely locate oneself, with respect to the person being addressed, with a pronoun in terms of age, status, kinship, gender, and situation. Some names are considered private because they are so closely identified with a person. Such private names would only be known by the closest relatives and acquaintances and used only in carefully regulated situations. Added to these are the English Christian names by which Native Americans are identified for official purposes by school and government officials. Even these names distinguish an aspect of the identity of Native American persons, an aspect often not of their choosing.

Practices associated with naming demonstrate the close association between the identity of a person and his or her names, and they also suggest the great complexity associated with personality and character. While names distinguish a person among a community, they also help shape and mold a person within the various communities and domains of culture in which this person must have a place, indeed, is known in terms of this place.

The formal practices that are engaged in starting the individual person on his or her road of life have a religious character. While these life-beginning occasions reflect beliefs about the nature of human existence and introduce the terms of one's destiny, they also create forms for the person, through which he or she may enter, not only into these beliefs, but also into the whole way of life with which they are identified. Naming is an important way of giving a person a meaningful destiny.[4]

RELIGIOUS AWARENESS THROUGH DISENCHANTMENT

As Hopi children attain the age of reason, around the ages of seven to ten, their first step into formal participation in the Hopi religious life is taken in their initiation into the kachina cult. Prior to their initiation, children are carefully protected from seeing kachina dancers without their masks in place, and from seeing any mask that is not being worn. Much effort is spent to create for the children a firm identity between the figures who appear as kachinas and the kachina spirits. From the children's point of view, the identity is obvious, for they have no basis for distinguishing the costume and mask from the persons wearing them. The uninitiated child's relationship with kachinas is close and extensive, and children frequently observe kachinas in their villages during more than six months of the year. They often receive gifts from these powerful and beautiful figures. They are told stories about them and they recognize them as perfect beings on whom depends the entire Hopi way of life. Some kachinas have a fearful appearance and threaten misbehaving children, frightening them into more acceptable and Hopi-like behavior. Children often imitate kachina dancing and emulate the high qualities identified with kachinas.

During the process of initiating the children into the kachina cult, the image that the children hold of the kachinas undergoes a severe transformation. The initiation rites occur during February in conjunction with the Powamu ceremony, which is the first major ceremonial in the kachina season. The children are taught many new things about their culture and especially about the origin and nature of kachina spirits. They undergo a ritual whipping, which serves as a reminder of the price they would pay if they revealed the secrets they have been told about the kachinas to the uninitiated. But the greatest effect of the initiation rites comes at the conclusion of Powamu during a dance in the kivas late at night. The newly initiated children are privileged to attend this dance for the first time. From within the kiva they hear the

Powamu kachinas approach and they see and hear the kachina father invite them into the kiva to dance. As the dancers descend the ladder into the kiva the newly initiated children observe that the kachinas are not what they had expected. In place of the beautiful kachina heads are human heads. Even worse, the children recognize the kachinas as their own male relatives. The immediate response of the children is often one of severe disenchantment, for the sudden recognition that the kachinas are masked impersonations threatens all that they have come to associate with the kachina figures. This leaves the Hopi children, at the threshold of a formal religious life, with serious doubts about the reality of the figures whom they had believed were essential to the Hopi way of life.

While it is clear that the Hopi consider this disenchantment to be a necessary stage in the religious development of the child, it is important not to assume that what the child learns is that kachinas are nothing more than impersonations. On the contrary, what is shown to the Hopi child through this disenchanting experience is that things are not simply what they appear to be. Reality includes much more than what one perceives with the eyes. It places the child in a position to learn what is perhaps the most important lesson in his or her entire religious life: that a spiritual reality is conjoined with and stands behind the physical reality. Certainly it is this realization that marks the beginning of religious awareness. For those who cannot comprehend this level of reality, the impersonation of kachinas could never be more than playacting. The experience of disenchantment strikes a deathblow to the naiveté that is characteristic of the uninitiated. The initiates can never return to that perspective again, for now they know what they could not even imagine before. This knowledge establishes an agenda of religious inquiry and a keen interest in pursuing it. The meaning of one's life depends on it. The induction of children through the passage into religious awareness is found in a variety of forms throughout North America.[5]

INITIATION AT PUBERTY

As the sun begins to rise, a beautifully dressed young Apache girl walks to the dancing ground to take her place on a buckskin in front of a singer and line of drummers. They all face toward the rising sun. She carries a cane crooked at one end and decorated with brightly colored ribbons and feathers. Facing the rising sun, the girl dances to songs that tell the story of Changing Woman, who, by her womanly powers of creativity, gave origin to the world as the Apache know it. As the girl dances, she prays that she might be given the creative powers of Changing Woman, the powers to continue the creation process of the Apache tradition. By the time the set of songs has ended, she has received these powers and in this way is transformed from a girl into a woman. She has acquired the role, the status, and the power that accompany the beginning of her menstruation, which she has recently experienced. The transformation is completed and celebrated in a four-day ceremony that follows, perhaps the grandest of Western Apache ceremonials. In Apache language it is called *na ih es,* which means "preparing her" or "getting her ready." In English it is called the Sunrise Dance.[6]

Preparations for the ceremony begin long before it is to be performed. The family sponsoring the ceremony must select and prepare a dance ground with various dwellings and cooking enclosures. Huge amounts of food must be acquired to feed the hundreds of guests who will attend. A medicine man must be found to sing the ceremony. A group of elders must be convened to plan the ceremony and advise the family on the proper procedures. A woman who will serve as model, teacher, and sponsor of the pubescent girl must be appointed. The ritual paraphernalia and costume must be prepared.

The four days before the ceremony begins are filled with preparations at the ceremonial grounds. Family and friends gather for the intense effort required to make it ready. During the evenings of these days of preparation dances last until around midnight. These major social occasions are attended by many. They feature lady's choice dancing, affording the girls a chance to make contact with eligible boys they admire.

On the day before the ceremony begins the ritual paraphernalia for the girl is prepared by her male relatives under the direction of the medicine man. All must purify themselves in a sweat lodge before they may engage in this important activity. The social dancing on the last evening before the ceremonial begins is the occasion for the first public appearance of the initiate. She appears in a buckskin dress of a Plains style with her ceremonial paraphernalia. The medicine man sings songs during this dance. The girl dances in a demure manner, in notable contrast to the gaiety of the other dancers.

Central to the ceremonial paraphernalia is the cane. It is a crooked staff made of hard wood so that it will not bend or break. It will serve this woman as an aid in walking when she reaches old age. It is decorated in a complex fashion, recalling cosmic orientations as well as factors related to the privileges and responsibilities of Apache womanhood. It is considered an agent of prayer and an instrument of spiritual mediation. The girl is also given a scratching stick because she must not touch her skin with her hands. Avoiding marring the skin emphasizes the importance of physical beauty. She is given a tube through which to drink. It is believed that if she touches water directly it would rain during her ceremonial.

To identify her with Changing Woman, a small pendant of abalone shell is tied to her hair so that it will hang on her forehead. One of the identities of Changing Woman is White Shell Woman. A pure white eagle feather is tied to her hair which, the Apache say, will cause her to live until her hair matches its color. Downy feathers are attached to her costume so that she may dance lightly.

On the morning of the first day of the ceremony, the pubescent girl becomes an Apache woman by means of her identification, described in a set of songs, with Changing Woman and the receipt of her powers. A second set is sung that recalls the event when Changing Woman was impregnated by the sun, a union whose offspring was a major culture hero of the Apache. The initiate physically identifies herself with Changing Woman during these songs by kneeling and facing the sun with her knees widespread in a symbolic posture of receiving the fertilizing rays of the sun. She sways from side to side with arms outstretched.

The next phase of the ceremony is the molding of the girl done by her model or sponsor. This woman, selected for her stature as an Apache woman, massages the girl as she lies on her buckskin. This act is done to give the girl the form of a woman. Once the massage is complete, the girl runs to the east, encircling her cane that has been erected at a distance. She runs to the east four times. Each time her cane is moved farther and farther away. The four runs are said to correspond with the four stages of life.

The girl runs to encircle her cane in each of the other cardinal directions, evoking the shape of the Apache world that appears throughout the ceremonial in many forms of number, color, and directional symbols. The girl's running assures her of a long and healthy life.

The four-day ceremony continues in a complex sequence of rituals. It is clear that in these rituals, as she becomes a woman, the Apache girl takes on a power as old as the Apache world itself. It is the power at the source of all creation. In her pubescence, she has become a creator, and through this ceremony she is made a bearer of the Apache tradition of creativity. The stages and ways of womanhood and life are revealed to her and she wins the promise for a long and fruitful life. By virtue of her identification with Changing Woman during the four days of the ceremony she acquires extraordinary creative power. She can cure the ill. She can bring rain. Many of the ritual acts during the ceremony use this power of Changing Woman for the benefit of the entire community. It is disseminated throughout the community by such acts as pouring many basketfuls of candy and treats over the girl's head. Contact with her makes the candy a vehicle for the transfer of power from the girl. The candy is highly sought after. Possessing it will assure plenty of food, a good crop of corn, or it may grant a wish.

Much more occurs in the Apache girls' puberty rite than a simple change in the social position and responsibility of a single female. It is far more than a declaration of her availability for marriage. While it is certainly both of these, it is also a renewal of the Apache community. The Apache worldview and way of life, as sanctioned in the stories of divine creation, are reaffirmed. Changing Woman is made present among the people once again and through the presence of her power the world is made anew.

Girls' puberty rites are common and widespread in North America west of the Rocky Mountains.[7] Almost without exception, the rites correspond with the onset of menstruation and they are usually performed for girls on an individual basis. The great differences in attitude about menstruation are clearly reflected in the way these rites are performed. Where menstruation is a condition of potential pollution to men, especially hunters or food producers, the initiate enters a period of isolation at the onset of menstruation. Isolation may last only for the duration of menstruation but it is often extended for a period of time, even up to a year. This period is a time for instruction, for self-reflection, and for preparation to be a woman. The seclusion is commonly ended with a feast or ceremony announcing the accession of the girl to womanhood.

While far fewer in number, some people, such as the Apache, associate the beginning of menstruation with the powers of creation. In this case, her presence brings health, beauty, newness, and a power to cure. Contact with her is sought, yet her potency may inspire a certain fear of her as well.

Among the most universal aspects of girls' puberty rites are taboos, restrictions, and special observations. These include a wide range of things such as hair styles, dress, posture, demeanor, work, rest, food, and bathing. Notably each of these is accompanied by a statement of what is thereby gained, avoided, or both. These ritual practices may be appreciated as an important way a culture articulates values, particularly those related to women. These ritual concerns show qualities and attributes both to be sought and avoided. The initiate bodily experiences these values.

Rites of initiating boys into manhood are not so precisely correlated with physiological maturity, perhaps because for males there is nothing so distinct as menstruation to indicate maturity. For males, initiation is often linked with accomplishments of food productivity, with the acquisition of a vision, or with the performance of some extraordinary physical feat. In many parts of North America, these markers pertain to females as well.[8]

THE VISION QUEST

The crushing experience of disenchantment may seem like harsh treatment for young people. But disenchantment may appear mild when we consider the widespread practice requiring children to enter periods of isolation during which they fast in pursuit of a vision experience. In some cultures this practice plays a central role in rites of initiation at puberty. For many cultures, the vision quest stands at the core of their religious traditions.

In the Great Lakes area Ojibwa culture, it was the practice to begin early in a child's life to prepare him or her for a vision fast. The parents implored their children to engage in short fasts to prepare them for receiving the power of a *manido,* or spiritual being. By age eight, a child might fast two meals every other day. Parents might awaken the child each morning by presenting the choice of eating bread or charcoal, and punishments for the child who chose bread encouraged the child to elect voluntary fasting. While religious awareness through the visionary experience was certainly momentous, it was not attained without much training and preparation. During the years of scheduled fasting, the child was made to think constantly about the power and guidance that he or she would receive in a vision.

The ceremonial fast occurred at puberty. While more attention was given to boys, Ojibwa girls were also expected to do a ceremonial fast at the time of first menstruation. Children were prepared for the ceremonial fast by being instructed on the importance of the event. They were told how to produce a vision and how to recognize and reject an evil vision. Knowledge of the way in which a vision informs one's life was considered essential for experiencing it properly, for the vision would not speak its wisdom wholly at the time it occurred. One had to live one's life according to the vision. In the process of living, the vision would reveal its powers through the good fortune, guidance, and protection it would direct toward the visionary.

At the proper time, as judged by an elder, the Ojibwa boy was led deep into the forest, where a lofty red pine tree was selected. On a high branch in this tree, was built a platform of woven sticks covered with moss as a bed on which the youth was to conduct the fast. Perhaps a canopy of branches would be prepared to shelter him from the wind and rain. Left alone in this place, the youth was strictly warned not to take any kind of nourishment or drink. He was to lie quietly day and night on this platform in a patient vigil for his vision. Elders might secretly check on the youth occasionally to give him aid if necessary. If the youth found that he could not endure the fast, he might return home, but he would then have to try again the following year. Further, if a boy had a bad dream or vision, he was instructed to give up his quest and return home to await another year. When visions rewarded the fast, they commonly took the form of a journey into the world of the spirits. During this journey the visionary was shown the path on which his life should proceed. He was associated with one or more spirit beings who would serve as his guardians and protectors throughout life. This association was given physical evidence in the revelation of certain objects that the visionary could procure as symbols of his spirit guardians.[9]

For the Ojibwa, religious awareness and the acquisition of spiritual powers come as products of a long, difficult period of preparation. Its significance is great. The process is one of educating children in the ways of their culture. They learn the roles, duties, and privileges of the adults they must soon become. They are shown how essential it is to live under the direction and protection of the *manido* or spirits. The vision quest prepares one physically and mentally to survive a life that may often be difficult. Receipt of a vision serves to establish one as an adult. It is a passageway that must be successfully navigated in order to enter adulthood with prestige and status.

Among many cultures in North America, religious awareness begins in the cultural process that culminates in a vision gained through an isolated fast. But the vision quest is not limited to the birth of religious awareness or to initiation at puberty, for it underlies a religious understanding of reality that is widespread in North America. It is an act performed in a wide variety of patterns. In a review of Plains tribes, Ruth Benedict found that the vision quest might be engaged on occasions of mourning, as an instrument of revenge on one's enemies, on account of a vow made in sickness or danger for oneself or one's relatives, on initiation into certain societies, and as a preparation for war. The vision quest must not be considered as associated only with the acquisition of what has commonly been termed a guardian spirit. The whole notion of the guardian spirit is itself diverse and is usually taken too simplistically. Guardian spirit is among a number of problematic theological categories that have been used to interpret Native American religious practices. Aside from such concerns, the vision quest often does not result in the acquisition of a guardian spirit or a spirit of any kind, but rather in the direct acquisition of power. Finally, the vision quest is not uniform in its procedures throughout North America and is not practiced at all among many cultures. Further, the use and significance to which the vision is put varies widely.[10]

Even with this great variety, common to the vision quest is a perception of reality in which the world of spiritual powers is essential to the successful fulfillment of human life. As the culture is given shape and meaning in terms of this fundamental understanding of reality, so too the individual person finds his or her identity, direction, guidance, protection, and destiny in terms of the awareness of this understanding of reality and engagement in it. It is at the core of personhood, joining the individual with a tradition and way of life, often integrating in the process the many domains of human experience and activity, from the banal and physical to the ethereal and mental. Because the vision quest is an individual event within the context of cultural expectations, the distinction and creativity of the individual within society is not sacrificed. Each person's identity and creativity is not only expressed but obtained through the vision experience and the powers to which it gives access. In some cultures like the Blackfeet, visions may be purchased, an act that gives the owner use of the ritual objects and words, which give access to certain spiritual powers. In this case, the possession of visions is, among other things, a display of wealth.

There are also other matters related to the vision quest: the distinction between visions and ordinary dreams, and the consistency of the symbolism found in the accounts by which Native Americans describe their vision experiences. There is general agreement that a true vision is distinguished by Native Americans from ordinary nighttime dreams or daydreams. Even the Yuman and Mohave people of Southern California and Arizona, whose nighttime dreams are central to their religious power and direction, distinguish between dreams of religious importance and ordinary dreams. Religious dreams seem to be of an entirely different character, and some individuals note that their dreams began even before they were born.

Still, while the vision or dream of extraordinary character has widespread importance in native North America, not every Native American is extraordinarily mystical and spiritual. As interesting as is the process of seeking a vision is the process that follows the vision experience. It is a process by which the abstract symbolic experience is examined, restructured, and ultimately transformed into a repeatable account of the vision experience. Only in the form of the dream story can such experiences be self-consciously used and shared with other members of the culture. In many Native American cultures, there is clearly a belief that the vision experience cannot be immediately understood. In Sioux cultures, for example, the abstract images and whatever can be described of the content of a vision experience must be told to the elders, who help the visionary understand the meaning of the experience. Here the vision experience is sought annually for four years and each vision is considered to complement and clarify the experiences previously received. The vision narrative may not be constructed to the point of being told for a long time. Black Elk, whose great vision is so well known through his telling of it to John G. Neihardt, did not tell his vision story to anyone for many years. Black Elk consulted the story as a guide to his life.[11]

This postvision process in no way reduces the importance of the momentous impact of the vision experience itself. Rather, it complements it by engaging contemplation and imagination in constructing a symbolic narrative out of the vision experience, fitting it into the meaningful context of one's life experiences and the tradition in which one lives.

The vision quest simultaneously serves the individual person and the cultural tradition in which he or she lives.

PILGRIMAGE

When physical geography is invested with religious significance, as is so common among Native Americans, physical movement can easily take on major significance. Shrines and physical features are significant to native cultures throughout North America. They are significant as world centers, world perimeters, markers of cardinal directions, the residences of spirits and gods, the transformed bodies of primordial figures, and doorways to the spiritual world. Some places are destinations of periodic pilgrimages, which enact historical or primordial dramas and serve to maintain the order and significance of the world. Some pilgrimage destinations may lie no farther than a shrine at the edge of the village or field, while others may be many days' journey to the peak of a distant mountain, the shores of a lake, or a shrine in the desert. The Papago pilgrimage for salt, though not undertaken for many years, remains in the memories of many Papago people.[12] The pilgrimage destination was the salt beds that form on the beaches in certain north shore areas of the Gulf of California. This destination is located almost directly west of the southern Arizona desert homes of the Papago people. Papago men took the pilgrimage in the summer on an annual basis. A youth might elect to attempt his first pilgrimage at the age of 16 or 17 after years of training for the arduous conditions he must endure. Once having decided to begin making pilgrimages, a man must participate for at least four successive years. Failure to do so might endanger his health. One is classified as a neophyte during the first four pilgrimages. Not until completing 10 or more pilgrimages is a man qualified to be a pilgrimage leader.

Before departing, pilgrims prepared their equipment, salt containers, canteens, food, and prayer sticks and corn meal for use as offerings. Many restrictions and procedures were carefully followed. More pertained to neophytes than to the seasoned pilgrims, called "ripe men." For example, a pilgrim must not step off the trail; he must not think of home or women; he must sleep with his head toward the ocean; he must not spill even a drop of water; he must speak slowly in a low voice or not at all. Neophytes must not walk but always run and they must eat only two meals a day.

The journey was taken over a seven-day period, carefully routed to lead the pilgrims past water sources and to certain locations for ritual observances. Each stop was the occasion for making offerings of prayer sticks and prayers. The evenings were spent with special ritual orations delivered by the leader to the pilgrims who sat in a circle. These orations recounted the significance of the journey and the goodness that would result from its proper completion. Prayers asked for strength to carry out the pilgrimage. The day before they reached the ocean, the pilgrims ran to the top of a mountain to gain their first sight of the ocean. Here they made offerings and ritually gestured to bring the power of the ocean toward them. Before they traveled on, they filled their canteens and drank their fill, for the next 24 hours had to be endured without water. Traveling during that night, the pilgrims had to camp close enough to the ocean so that on the following day they could reach the ocean and return to this camp, where they would retrieve their canteens.

The next morning they traveled on to the ocean. Finding the salt deposit about a half-mile from the shore, they ran four times around the one-quarter of a mile long salt bed before gathering the salt. Then they ran the half-mile to the ocean, wading into it with offerings of prayer sticks and corn meal, strewing them upon the first four waves. Having made these offerings, the pilgrims ran along the beach as far as they wanted to go. They did not look back until they were ready to turn around and run back. It was during this run that the pilgrims experienced personal visions. These visions, according to the stories told of them, were often associated with things the runner saw, such as birds, shells, and seaweed. Objects associated with the visions were considered to be invested with power and they were picked up by the runners. The visions commonly foretold events in the lives of the pilgrims.

After returning to the salt beds they gathered and loaded the salt, which had dried during the day, on horses to be carried back to their homes. On their return, they approached the village in the evening, but, as after a war party, they did not enter it. This permitted some of the villagers to come meet them. Young boys came toward them whirling bull-roarers in imitation of the thunder associated with the rain the pilgrims were understood to be bringing from the ocean. Old women came to collect gifts of salt.

On their return, the pilgrims, especially the neophytes, were isolated for a period of time while the acquired effects of the power of the ocean gradually left them, making them safe to engage once again in normal social activities. The pilgrim was isolated during this period in a special enclosure. He was given new dishes from which to eat. Every four days, his dishes were "killed" by having holes knocked in their bottoms, and new ones were given to him.

During this period of isolation the fathers of eligible girls might approach the parents of the unmarried neophytes to offer their daughters in marriage.

The pilgrimage is a complicated ritual process. At one level, it serves as a rite of passage from youth to manhood. This passage is based on the performance of a feat requiring the strength of a man, the acquisition of supernatural power through contact with the ocean, and on the visions gained during the pilgrimage. It culminates a childhood of physical and spiritual preparation. It initiates manhood and family life.

Yet religious processes that focus on the individual person often also serve the life of the entire community. For the whole community the salt pilgrimage seeks life itself. For it is through the pilgrimage to the ocean and the collection of salt that the deity in control of rain is persuaded to release this life-giving substance. The pilgrims bring back not only salt but also rain. Symbolically, the pilgrimage draws a parallel between the interrelationship of corn and rain and the interrelationship of salt and the ocean. During the pilgrimage, salt is referred to as corn. This is part of the ritual language of pilgrims. By going to the ocean, one goes to the source of rain water. Indeed, the rain clouds in late summer come from the gulf to the Papago people, and these approaching clouds denote the coming of a new year. By bringing back the salt deposited by the ocean, a substance itself vital to life in the desert, the pilgrims bring refreshing vitalizing rain, that is, new life to the Papago world.

This level of significance in the pilgrimage is expressed beautifully in the many pilgrimage ritual orations.

> The remains of a cigarette did I place upright.
> I put it to my lips,
> I smoked.

> To the rain house standing in the west I came.
> All kinds of mist were bound up there,
> And I could not (unbind them).
> It was my cigarette smoke.
> Circling around it, it entered and unbound them.
> I tried to see him, my guardian [lit., "made father"]
> But squarely turned away from me he sat.
> It was my cigarette smoke.
> Circling around, it turned him toward me.

> Thus I spoke, to him, my guardian.
> "What will happen?
> Most wretched lies the earth which you have made.
> The trees which you have planted, leafless stand.
> The birds you threw into the air,
> They perch and do not sing.
> The springs of water are gone dry.
> The beasts which run upon the earth,

They make no sound."
Thus I said.
"What will befall the earth which you have made?"
Then, thus spake he, my guardian,
"Is this so difficult?
You need but gather and recite the ritual.
Then, knowing all is well,
Go to your homes."

Then back I turned.
Eastward, I saw, the land was sloping laid.
Slowly along I went.
I reached my former sleeping place and laid me down.
Thus, four days did I travel toward the east.
Then in the west a wind arose,
Well knowing whither it should blow.
Up rose a mist and towered toward the sky,
And others stood with it, their tendrils touching.
Then they moved.

Although the earth seemed very wide,
Clear to the edge of it did they go.
Although the north seemed very far,
Clear to the edge of it did they go.
Then to the east they went, and, looking back,
They saw the earth lie beautifully moist and finished.

Then out flew Blue Jay shaman;
Soft feathers he pulled out and let them fall.
The earth was blue (with flowers).
Then out flew Yellow Finch shaman;
Soft feathers he pulled out and let them fall,
Till earth was yellow (with flowers).
Thus was it fair, our year.

Thus should you also think,
All you my kinsmen.

(Underhill et al., *Rainhouse and Ocean,* pp. 66–67. Used by permission.)

Pilgrimage is a difficult and dangerous journey. The destination is not one frequented or ever seen by anyone other than pilgrims. It is beyond the space perceived by the ordinary person and therefore is a potent or strong place. The extraordinary character of the pilgrimage is marked by such things as special rules and restrictions, ritual language, and ritual procedures. The climactic moment comes when the destination is gained. The substance of power and the resulting transformations are effected here. Although first an affair of individual persons, the pilgrimage process forms a camaraderie among the pilgrims, a unity and power that, upon their return, is ritually disseminated to the entire community. The pilgrimage transforms the pilgrim from youth to adult and from religious naiveté to vision-directed maturity. It also transforms the community, even effecting a new year.

HEALTH AND HEALING

In the Pueblo village of Cochiti near the Rio Grande River in New Mexico, a person who is ill may ask to be treated by a medicine society. This is usually done when one fears that one's illness is the result of witchcraft. The medicine society whose help is sought spends four days in its society house preparing for the arduous task that lies ahead. The medicine men go to the house of the sufferer and the ensuing ritual cure builds in a four-day crescendo of events. The sick person is the focus of this affair, during which much singing, praying, and smoking are directed toward his or her recovery. The medicine society must pit its ritual powers against the forces of witchcraft and the force of this battle and the fear related to the potential consequences build dramatically. A climax is reached on the fourth night when the threatening presence of witches is felt everywhere and it becomes clear that the strengths being mustered by the medicine society must be great enough to overcome the powers of the witches. On the fourth night, a painting in corn meal is made on the floor. Lines of meal are strewn to connect the picture with the doorway of the house. After dark, the medicine men of the society begin to sing as they enter, carrying objects associated with the sources of their healing powers, such as figurines of deities and animals. Wearing only a breechcloth and with his face painted, each medicine man proceeds along one of the roads of meal and places his power object upon the meal painting. This meal painting represents the collective medicine powers whose forces are invoked in these ritual procedures.

Into a medicine bowl, water is poured from the six directions and each medicine man adds medicinal herbs to the water. Each medicine man then approaches the sick person, rubs his or her body with ashes, and performs a divining examination in the attempt to locate witch objects in the person's body that have been "shot" there by a malevolent being, a witch. When these objects are "seen," the medicine men ritually suck them from the body and spit them in a bowl for all to see as evidence of the cure.

The curing process also attracts witches who attempt to win over the sick person from the medicine society and bring harm to the medicine men. Though warriors armed with bows and arrows are stationed around the house, witches may still intrude. They make their terrifying presence known by knocking at the doors and windows and by making horrid calls in the darkness.

Witches may harm people by means other than "shooting" objects of witchery into them. They may steal a person's heart, the center of vitality. When the medicine society determines that this is the case, the medicine men have no choice but to attempt a rescue of the heart. They must enter the witches' domain, the darkness of night, and do battle with them in order to recover the stolen heart. Leaving the home of the sick person, the medicine men run into the surrounding darkness. Invested with medicine power, they may even fly. The noises of fierce battle are heard. Sometimes a medicine man returns battered and bloody from his combat. Medicine men overcome in these ritual battles may be found tied tightly with wire. But with great effort, the medicine men will overcome a witch and bring it squealing back to the fireside where, in the shadows, it is shot with arrows and killed. The witch is often a small figure in either human or animal form. The stolen heart, in the form of a kernel of corn, is recovered from a bundle of rags. It is given to the sick person to swallow, thus effecting the cure. After sharing food with everyone present, the society of medicine men gathers its paraphernalia and departs.[13]

Witchcraft[14] is but one of the causes of illness recognized by the Cochiti who attribute other illnesses to natural causes. These are treated with herbal medicines and ordinary means of rendering aid, including treatment by Western medicine in a hospital. A third kind of illness is distinguished because of its tendency to persist. This type, not attributed to witchcraft, is treated by a process that effects initiation into a clan. In this way, a person may extend his or her social relationships, an act viewed as a way of procuring good health and guarding against bad health.

Simply from the way in which the Cochiti perceive the nature of health and the processes by which they approach healing and the maintenance of good health, the conditions of one's health may speak of meanings that transcend a set of physiological, biological, and psychological factors. Health is not perceived as a condition confined to the individual. While in some cases sickness is simply a sign of one or more individual factors, it just as commonly reflects the conditions of a broader social and cultural environment and even the conditions of the spiritual world.

In the Cochiti view, the world exists in the precarious interplay between the forces of the *shiwana* and of witchcraft and malevolence. *Shiwana* are various deities and spirit beings who serve the world by establishing conditions of fertility, nurturance, and good health. They do not dominate and control the world, thus the Cochiti people must call on them and engage them in life-giving relationships. Order is threatened by the forces of witchcraft aimed at bringing ill health, bad relations, infertile conditions, and disruptive social relationships. Witches are manifest in many forms such as humans, animals, birds, and even fireballs. In the Cochiti view, the world is a battleground on which these two forces struggle eternally. Neither can dominate more than temporarily. The oscillatory struggle between polar forces constitutes the vitalizing force of Cochiti life.

Witchcraft is a subject that runs throughout many Cochiti oral traditions attesting the extent to which it influences the entire Cochiti way of life. Clearly it is a constant factor in social relations, in one's attitudes toward oneself and others, in an individual's perception of his or her place in the family, society, and whole Cochiti world.

With only this scant description of the religious thought of the Cochiti as background, the curing rituals can be understood. The medicine society is engaged in nothing short of enacting cosmic processes. It spends time preparing for and invoking the forces of the *shiwana* through prayers, songs, offerings, the use of figurines, shamanic techniques of divination and witch-object extraction, ritual battles, and a host of symbolic patterns that choreograph and coordinate the many ritual acts into a unified, strongly significant event.

Matters of maintaining health are a major part of the religion of many Native American cultures. Yet, perhaps because at some levels they appear to conflict so sharply with the practice of Western scientific medicine, these aspects of Native American religions have been greatly misunderstood or considered to be primitive psychology or primitive pharmacopoeia. This failure to understand becomes especially damning in any attempt to understand a Native American religion such as the Navajo, whose whole world centers on religious views of health. To a remarkable degree the Cochiti and Navajo focus on health as the core of their highly complex religious traditions. While health may be concerned with the individual sufferer, being motivated by and directly serving the felt needs of the individual, matters of health and healing are also how Native Americans create and effect worldview and social relationships. Health and healing are means by which Native Americans create and align themselves with the order and meaningfulness of their world. In Native American cultures, the condition of one's health is the simultaneous barometer of the status or condition of the place on which one stands and the symbolic language used to gauge and express that status or condition. It also serves to reorient the individual and the whole social complex to affect these conditions.

THE JOURNEY'S END

In her beautifully poignant short story "The Man to Send Rain Clouds," the Laguna Pueblo writer Leslie Silko describes the events at the end of the old man Teofilo's life. When his children find him dead at a sheep camp, they paint his face and tie a small feather in his hair. There was a smile on his son's face as he strewed corn meal and pollen in the wind and bade his father to send rain clouds.[15] In even this minor aspect of the funeral rite of passage is revealed the Pueblo belief in the interdependence of the living and the dead. If one lives a proper life into old age, he will become a cloud or kachina spirit in death. These spiritual entities, then, are identified with the life-giving substance rain. For many cultures in North America, the journey along life's road does not end in death but continues beyond this life and world. For the Pueblo and other people, the afterlife remains in intimate interrelationship with the world of the living. Hence, there is an affinity between the dead and the spiritual world. Many other cultures identify the dead with potentially malevolent ghosts and witches.

Common in North America are descriptions of human destiny, the goal of life, as living a life of good health leading to a death in old age. Death in old age is not the result of an imbalance in cosmic forces or the final failure of efforts to ward off ill health, but rather a passage that has been prepared for throughout the journey along life's road. With death in advanced age as life's goal, a premature death is often understood as a matter for serious concern. Consistent with Native American religious views of health, the occasion of death speaks not only of the plight and destiny of the deceased but of the status of the world in which the person has lived and died. Death before old age may be considered a time of grave danger, of high suspicion aimed even at members of the family and community, and of self-contemplation by the living about the conditions that led to this death.

Funeral rites are rites of passage, for they resolve the state of impropriety that arises at death: the presence of a dead person in the domain of the living. The rite resolves this condition by inducting the deceased into the domain of the dead. This is a particularly important religious occasion, for, whatever the status of the dead, a funeral rite of passage necessarily involves the contact of the two distinct spheres, the living and the dead. The occasion of death, therefore, affords a religious community the opportunity to address such things as eschatology, that is, final and ultimate things, and destiny. There is most certainly a religious aspect to all funeral and mortuary customs. Consequently it is possible to infer something of the religious beliefs of prehistoric people from burials.

Death is a major subject in Native American oral traditions. Stories that deal with various aspects of death include the origin of death, visits by mortals to the land of the dead, and the journey by a husband to the land of the dead in search of his dead wife. This latter story is of particular interest because of its widespread incidence in North America and its identification with the classical Greek story of Orpheus and Eurydice.[16]

For life's road to be meaningful, it must lead somewhere, it must have a destination. Death is either the event of life's ultimate fulfillment or an occasion for religious concern and reorientation. Few moments in the life of the individual can rival the moment of death for bearing religious significance.

CONCLUSION

It has become clear that many aspects of the religions of Native American people are focused on the individuals. In Native American cultures the religious aspects of life's road are central. The word individual is commonly used to indicate a person set against society. Individual freedom is usually thought of in terms of the degree to which one stands apart from society.

Yet, for many Native Americans this opposition of individual and society is not the case. While persons are subjects of numerous formal religious events throughout their lives, these religious events serve also to integrate them into society and the traditions that give it common identity and meaning. It is, perhaps, more fitting to refer to the Native American as person rather than individual, in order to emphasize attributes of identity, character, value, and role rather than to designate a unit distinct from the collective. The Native American person is often given identity, nurturance, direction, and motivation in the process of becoming integrated with society. While freedom for Native American persons is definable only in societal terms, this freedom is nonetheless present.

Native American roads of life may be seen as a sequence of passages that conduct persons from stage to stage throughout life. They must also be seen as processes of the introduction and accumulation of knowledge, techniques, responsibilities, privileges, and relationships sanctioned by the religious character that sustains and gives life meaning.

NOTES

1. Don Talayesva, *Sun Chief: The Autobiography of a Hopi Indian* (New Haven: Yale University Press, 1942), p. 25.

2. Ruth Bunzel, *Zuni Ritual Poetry,* Smithsonian Institution, Bureau of American Ethnology, 47th Annual Report (Washington, D.C., 1929), p. 635.

3. N. Scott Momaday, *The Names: A Memoir* (New York: Harper and Row, 1976), unnumbered page preceding p. 1.

4. For examples of naming practices, see George A. Pettitt, *Primitive Education in North America* (Berkeley: University of California Press, 1946), pp. 59–74.

5. For further discussion, see Sam D. Gill, "Hopi Kachina Cult Initiation: The Shocking Beginning to the Hopi's Religious Life," *Journal of the American Academy of Religion* XLV2 Supplement (1977): A:447–64.

6. Keith Basso, *The Gift of Changing Woman,* Smithsonian Institution, Bureau of American Ethnology Bulletin no. 196 (Washington, D.C., 1966), pp. 113–73.

7. See Harold E. Driver, *Girls' Puberty Rites in Western North America,* Anthropological Records Series (Berkeley: University of California Press, 1941).

8. See George A. Pettitt, *Primitive Education in North America* (Berkeley:

University of California Press, 1946), pp. 40–58, 87–104 for further examples.

9. For descriptions, see Ruth Landis, *The Ojibwa Woman* (New York: Columbia University Press, 1938), pp. 1–16; and for vision stories, see J. G. Kohl, *Kitchi-Gami* (1860; reprint ed., Minneapolis: Ross and Haines, 1956), pp. 204–42.

10. See Ruth F. Benedict, "The Concept of the Guardian Spirit in North America," *American Anthropological Association Memoirs* 29 (1923); and Ruth F. Benedict, "The Vision in Plains Culture," *American Anthropologist* 24 (1922): 1–23.

11. John G. Neihardt, *Black Elk Speaks* (Lincoln: University of Nebraska Press, 1961), pp. 20–47.

12. See Ruth Underhill, *Papago Indian Religion* (New York: Columbia University Press, 1946), pp. 211–42; and Ruth Underhill et al., *Rainhouse and Ocean: Speeches for the Papago Year* (Flagstaff: Museum of Northern Arizona Press, 1979), pp. 37–70.

13. See J. Robin Fox, "Witchcraft and Clanship in Cochiti Therapy," in *Magic, Witchcraft and Curing,* ed. John Middleton (Austin: University of Texas Press, 1967), pp. 255–84.

14. The English terms associated with witchcraft are often used by Native Americans and, thus, used here. Still it

must be remembered that each Native American language has its own terms to refer to malevolence and malevolent beings. With the recent awareness of the positive intentions of such groups as wicans, for example, the term witch has become subject of renewed sensitivity, concerns not yet acknowledged in common use.

15. Leslie M. Silko, "The Man to Send Rain Clouds," in *The Man to Send Rain Clouds: Contemporary Stories by American Indians,* ed. Kenneth Rosen (New York: Viking, 1974), pp. 3–8.

16. See Ake Hultkrantz, *North American Indian Orpheus Tradition* (Stockholm: The Ethnographical Museum of Sweden, 1957).

6

Ways of Life

At Hopi in northern Arizona when the sun reaches a certain place on the horizon in springtime, people gather in their fields some distance from the villages. The men enter a shade, a partial enclosure, where they smoke and offer prayers. Then, after placing prayer sticks on the ground before a shrine at the edge of each field, the leader of the planting party takes a handful of corn meal and sprinkles it about the shrine in the six ritual directions as he prays for rain and good crops.

The subsequent planting is performed in a ritually defined manner with each specified act associated either with the hope of avoiding some disaster or with some encouraged benefit. Planting is but one step in a series of activities that engage the Hopi in an annual cycle. Few of the countless ritual acts that constitute the Hopi way of life do not involve corn in one form or another. Corn is an inextricable part of the Hopi way of life.

The Naskapi of the Labrador peninsula are hunting people. In the spring, they go to the dens of bears just as they emerge from hibernation. Standing before the den they address the bear as grandfather or grandmother and apologize for their need to kill it. They thank it for giving its flesh that they might be sustained in life. After killing the bear, they place tobacco in its mouth and proceed with the butchering and the distribution of meat in a ritually prescribed manner. The bear skull is decorated with paint and mounted on a pole or suspended from a tree where it serves as an important ritual object for the people during the following year. The Naskapi religious beliefs and ritual practices, their whole way of life, revolves around hunting and in the animals that sustain life.

In spring, at the time of catching the first salmon or gathering the first acorns, the foods that most sustained the native people in northwest California, an extended ceremonial was performed. Although it took a variety of complex and extensive forms among the several people who lived in that area, it was generally performed for the purpose of making the earth firm, celebrating the first fruits, extinguishing the old fires and kindling a new fire, and preventing disease and calamity in the year to come. In short, these rites, so closely associated with the foods that sustained the people, amounted to what anthropologist Alfred Kroeber called world renewal.[1] The way of life, indeed the whole world, originated in the vital association with the first fruits harvested from the streams and surrounding lands.

Environmental factors have usually been considered as constraints in the study of Native American cultures. People are restricted by the climate and terrain in which they live and by the type and availability of food resources. These ecological factors have been recognized as shaping the development of social relationships, technology, art, and religion. Although this view is certainly useful, an alternative perspective is more fruitful when considering Native American religions.

Environmental elements, no matter how commonplace or simple, are grasped by Native Americans with an imagination that transforms mere surface appearances into vehicles for creating and enacting their conceptions of reality and human existence. The banal becomes special.

As expected, Native Americans use elements of their common daily sustenance activities in the religious processes by which they come to terms with one another, with reality, and with the origin, meaning, and destiny of being human. If one is a hunter living on the flesh of animals, equipped with tools and sheltered by structures made of animal bones and skins, it is scarcely surprising that one's religion is built around animals' habitats and characteristics, the hunt, and the interrelationship between hunter and hunted. The religions of fishers and farmers likewise reflect their modes of sustenance.

BEAR CEREMONIALISM

Since human beings first appeared on earth, perhaps two million years ago, they have sustained themselves primarily by hunting and gathering. Agriculture was discovered as a possible mode of sustaining human cultures only about 10,000 years ago, and few cultures that in time became agricultural gave up hunting entirely. Scant evidence exists of the religious beliefs and practices of most human beings throughout human prehistory. The surviving prehistoric evidence reveals only dim shadows of these early religions. Yet it seems clear that early religions were closely associated with hunting activities. Caves in

Europe have yielded evidence that humans who hunted bears as early as the Upper Paleolithic gave special attention to the treatment of the bones of their game. They placed the leg bones through the cheek arches of the skulls and carefully oriented the skulls in caches in their cave dwellings. While these events occurred geographically far from America, they are nonetheless important because the religious practices of many circumpolar hunting people, including those in North America, often center on the bear and frequently include ritual treatment of the bear carcass and bones. Scholars considering the widespread incidence of bear ceremonialism and its correlation with artifactual evidence datable from early human times have concluded that bear ceremonialism is perhaps among the oldest forms of religious practice.[2]

More contemporary examples are similar in some respects. Numerous groups of the Algonquin people occupy eastern Canada from the area between the Great Lakes and Hudson Bay eastward through Labrador. Included are the Eastern Cree, numerous bands of Ojibwa, and the Montagnais and Naskapi, as well as the Eskimo to the north. Throughout this area, bears of various kinds were sought as a major source of food. Bear hunting was conducted according to complex religious procedures. While the hunting rites varied in detail from group to group, a fairly representative picture can be drawn of the hunting ceremonials of the Northern Saulteaux, an Ojibwa people.

Among the Northern Saulteaux, the black bear was given most consideration. Treatment of the bear approached the level of veneration. In hunting the bear, special procedures were carefully followed. A hunter would not kill a bear until he had first addressed it, using a specified name or kinship designation. In this address, the hunter apologized for having to kill the bear, explaining that it was only because of his great hunger and his people's need for food. He would plead with the bear not to become angry, a concern not for the hunter's safety but rather for the continuing presence of bears to provide for the people's needs. The kill was accomplished only with a war club or a knife. Upon killing the bear, the hunter immediately dressed it in fine clothing so that it took on the appearance of a human being. The Saulteaux explanation for this practice is notable.

> [T]he bears have a king, or chief, and the orders of this chief must be obeyed. Sometimes he orders a bear to go to an Indian trap. When a dead bear is dressed up it is done as an offering or prayer to the chief of the bears to send more of his children to the Indians. If this were not done, the spirit of the bear would be offended and would report the circumstances to the chief of bears who would prevent the careless Indians from catching more.[3]

Beyond this honoring of the bear, the Saulteaux also erected a pole where they hung the skull, the skin of the bear's muzzle, and its ears. Offerings of tobacco and ribbons were also hung on the pole. This ritually prepared pole was left standing when the hunters moved on, as a sign of the hunters' respect for the slain bear and for the chief or owner of the animal species. In these ritual acts they assured the continuity of the supply of game and their success in hunting.

The butchering and distribution of flesh was conducted according to ritual prescription. The hunter cut a small piece of the heart to be offered to the spiritual owner of the bears and consumed the remainder himself hoping to acquire the cunning and courage of the bear. The tongue and heart were not to be eaten by women. The bones were not given away or left to be eaten by dogs. They were placed on platforms in trees for their protection.

Hunting rituals are also performed for other animals by the Northern Saulteaux and other people of this area. At their camp, hunters frequently erected a staff on which they displayed the skulls or heads of the animals and birds they pursued.[4]

This abbreviated description of hunting rites raises two interesting topics. First is the treatment of the bear and other animals as though they were persons, and second is the belief in a chief or owner of an animal species. Both are widespread and common among Native American hunting people.

Hunting people in this and other areas consider bears to be equal in intelligence to humans and capable of understanding everything that is said to them. The religious relationship of hunters and game is often forged through speech. Honored hunters can talk to and understand animals. How is this purported discourse to be comprehended and how might it serve to enhance the understanding of Native American religions?

A. I. Hallowell, pursuing this matter in the context of Ojibwa culture, gained important insights.[5] Hallowell found that the Ojibwa category person provides a major key to understanding the Ojibwa worldview. The category person in Western conceptions normally refers only to human beings, but Hallowell found that this restriction does not hold for the Ojibwa. It is a category that extends throughout the material and spiritual world. Still, the Ojibwa are not animatists. They do not simply perceive everything in the world as invested with life. Hallowell demonstrated this by recounting the response made by an Ojibwa who appeared to consider rocks as sentient. When asked if *all* rocks are alive, he responded "No. But *some* are."[6] At the base of the Ojibwa worldview is the understanding that anything has the possibility of being perceived and treated on a person-to-person basis. This designation of the category person constitutes an important difference between Ojibwa and European-American views of reality. To be properly understood, hunting rituals must be considered in terms of the worldview of the people performing them.

For the Northern Saulteaux, for example, there is a correlation between their perception of the hunting situation and their conduct. When in contact with game animals, the Saulteaux are confronted with animate beings who have not only the attributes of a bear or other animal but also the attributes of a person. These attributes are not seen as one inside the other but as aspects of an integral whole.

In his consideration of the Ojibwa understanding of the category person, Hallowell found that a crucial distinction was made between human beings and other-than-human beings. Hallowell maintains that it is misleading to correlate this Ojibwa distinction with the Western religious distinction of natural and supernatural because the Ojibwa have little notion of the ordered regularity of movement or of a set of *impersonal* natural laws by which the world operates. Causes and effects in the world result from the actions of persons, both human and other-than-human. In the absence of the notion of nature, at least in the scientific sense of the word, the corresponding term supernatural cannot be a meaningful designation in the Ojibwa view of the world. The common stereotypical notion that Native Americans are people at one with nature and, at the same time, wholly connected with the supernatural is questionable.

The second issue raised by the Northern Saulteaux example is the belief in a chief or owner of animals. This belief has great antiquity and is found among hunting people the world over. Hallowell found that the distinction between human and other-than-human persons correlated in the Ojibwa view with the capability of persons to undergo metamorphosis. Humans are much less capable of undergoing metamorphosis than are other-than-human beings. Life is possible because of the possession of two aspects, one identified with the spiritual soul or eternal life force, the other with the appearances one may take, which are temporal and subject to change either gradually or suddenly. These conceptions underlie the belief in the regeneration of animals from season to season and are doubtless associated with the care given to the bones, which are identified with the seat of the animal's vitality. Properly honored and cared for, these bones representing the animals' eternal source of vitality may undergo metamorphosis by regenerating flesh contributing to the cycle of reciprocity by which humans and animals interrelate and depend on one another for life. The conception of the chief or owner of the animal species gives concrete expression to this life-giving interrelationship between humans and game animals. The Northern Saulteaux envision the owner of the bears as a bear of extraordinary size with remarkable spiritual powers.

These principles also underlie the beliefs about witchcraft and other nefarious activities. The danger of such things is related to the capacity of a malintentioned person to undergo metamorphosis, to change his or her appearance. Widespread are stories told of persons who take on the appearance of bears as the guise in which they pursue their awful deeds. Such persons are known as bearwalkers.[7]

Importantly, the commonplace elements of the sustenance activities are not seen simply as food and nourishment but as images of the nature of reality and human existence. For the Northern Saulteaux, a bear is not simply a large, furry animal that supplies meat, tools, and hide. It is a person with whom one must maintain a proper relationship. This relationship not only assures bodily survival, but also serves as the foundation for all of life's meaning. Such beliefs and practices form the core of the religions of these hunting people. Within the broad pattern of the religious beliefs and practices of hunters there is much variety.

THE BLADDER FESTIVAL
OF THE ALASKAN ESKIMO

Central to an Alaskan Eskimo festival, the bladders of all the birds and animals slain during the year are inflated, painted, and hung in the men's society house. These odd-shaped balloons are identified with or symbolize the souls of the game animals. The bladder festival, well known throughout Alaskan coastal areas, honors these slain animals as well as the hunters. At the conclusion of the festival, the souls of the animals as represented by the bladders are symbolically returned to their place of origin so that they may regenerate and return once again as game to the hunters.

As with those hunters of the eastern and northern regions of North America an entire continent apart, the hunting ideology is associated with the return and regeneration of the game animals. The bladders are treated in a manner similar to the skulls and bones of the bears. But this is to consider only the surface similarities. The Alaskan Eskimo performances of the bladder festival are the fabric into which are woven the many concerns of the specific religious community.

On Nunivak Island, for example, the bladder festival is performed annually over a period of many days. It begins with a sweatbath for all the men followed by a dance and a feast during which the men give their wives valuable gifts. Ritual restrictions characterize the following several days of preparation. The women make new clothing for everyone and the men make new dishes, decorated in patterns commemorating the great hunting feats of the year. The men also create new songs, which they all learn for singing later.

On the particular evening when the festival begins, all fires and lights are extinguished. While songs are sung, a shaman performs a ritual journey to the homes of the animals and their spiritual owners where he repairs relationships with the game owners and consults them about the availability of game for the coming hunting season.

The next morning the men dress in their new clothes and turn their attention to the upcoming spring hunting season. As the dishes that the men have carved are collected, each man sings songs that tell of the feats commemorated in the designs painted on the dishes. The children of the hunters will eat from these dishes during the festival, enacting through the banal act of eating the interdependence of food, hunter, hunt, and game.

Solemnity reins for a time once the inflated bladders are hung in the men's ceremonial house. The bladders, symbolizing the souls of the game, must not be left unguarded. A fire is kept constantly burning in the house and no sharp noises or unexpected actions are tolerated for fear of frightening away the game associated with the bladders.

The bladders are honored for a period of four days. Every evening all of the village people gather in the ceremonial house. The men don their wooden hunting hats or animal heads and imitate, in song and dance, the feats of courage they have accomplished during the year. A feast is enjoyed each evening following this performance. On the last night, a shaman enters the sea through a hole cut in the ice. This time he journeys to the spiritual world of the sea animals. Later the shaman reappears at the skylight and tells the people the events of his journey.

Also on the last night of the bladder festival, five holes are made in the ice in front of the village. A fire is made there as well. After elaborate preparations in the ceremonial house, each hunter takes his own animal bladders outside. The caribou and bird bladders are placed on the fire, and the seal bladders are punctured and placed in the sea through the ice holes. This action symbolizes the return of the souls of the game to their spirit homes. The village people gather by families around the fire and softly sing the hunting songs, which are passed from generation to generation in each family. This singing concludes in the morning when the men take a sweatbath to remove the taboos and restrictions they have observed. All enjoy a final feast.[8]

Even in this brief description of one bladder festival, the wide range of religious factors is apparent. It is foremost a rite of the new year. The old year and its activities are commemorated, retold, honored, and set aside with the old clothing, old dishes, and bladders of the slain animals as the new year is initiated. Indeed, the honor paid the bladders presages the coming hunting season, as does the making of new clothing and dishes. The old year is interdependent with the coming year in the same way that the game animals and hunters are interdependent. This festival gives definition and meaning to the entire social structure, gender roles, clan organizations, age levels, work, food, everything. It is also a period of passage along the life cycle, serving as a time for the initiation of boys into manhood, which is celebrated by their formal entrance into the men's ceremonial house and their first participation in the festival rites. The bladder festival is a major ceremonial not only for the transmission of religious traditions but also for maintaining the structures of meaning within those traditions.

THE KWAKIUTL WINTER CEREMONIAL

On a winter night the members of various religious societies of the Kwakiutl people of the Pacific Northwest Coast perform dances in the Winter Ceremonial lodge. By dancing, members of perhaps the most important religious society, known as *hamatsa,* attempt to lure back to the ceremonial lodge a youth who, some days earlier, was caught and devoured by the great god "Man Eater at the North End of the World." The youth, who is undergoing initiation into the *hamatsa* or devourer society, does not return. At dawn, the members of the *hamatsa* society begin dancing again trying to bring back the youth. In the lodge, corpses, skulls, and worms are ever-present symbols of death. As they dance around the fire singing the dance-of-death song, the *hamatsa* utter the cry "hap, hap," "eat, eat," in imitation of their tutelary, Man Eater. Suddenly a noise is heard on the roof. The shingles are torn loose and a wild figure drops to the floor of the lodge. It is the youth now transformed by the Man Eater. He is clothed only in garlands of pine branches. His face is blackened and bleeding. The dancers rush at him, but he wrenches free of them and flees through the door.

The dancers quickly erect a pole, representing Man Eater, protruding through the roof of the lodge. A screen with a hole cut in it and painted to represent the mouth of Man Eater is set up in the lodge.

The youth, transformed into a man eater, soon returns and climbs up the pole and out of the lodge. Again he enters the lodge through the door and this time the dancers succeed in catching him. The whole society engages in the man-eating activities of their tutelary by pantomiming the eating of a human corpse. The initiate, slightly calmed by this cannibal act, is again devoured by Man Eater, enacted by the youth going into his mouth, the hole in the screen. The *hamatsa* dancers gradually calm themselves by going to bathe in the sea and again attempt to bring back the youth. Through the use of seawater and eagle-down feathers, both symbolizing wealth and life, the initiate is brought back to be treated further. He emerges through the mouth of the god as if regurgitated. Finally upon crawling four times through a wreath of cedar, also representing the mouth of Man Eater, the initiate is calmed or, as the Kwakiutl say, healed and thus becomes a member of the *hamatsa* society.[9] This is but one of many ritual scenarios that form part of the Winter Ceremonial.

The Kwakiutl live along the coastal region between Vancouver and Alaska. Their coastline homeland includes thousands of islands and fjords that bring the sea far inland. The abundant rain nourishes the forest areas enclosing their villages on the landward side. An abundance of food is available through both hunting and fishing. The Kwakiutl are noted for their massive wooden houses constructed along a street bordering the shore and the distinctively carved totem poles.

The religious beliefs and ceremonial expressions of the Kwakiutl and other Pacific Northwest Coast cultures are as complex and highly developed as anywhere in North America. Kwakiutl religious traditions are also shaped by concern for the relationship between human beings and the animals on whom they depend for life, though this concern is perhaps not so obvious as in other hunting people. The long, spectacular Winter Ceremonial and the practice of potlatching, that is, the ritual distribution of goods, are essential to the Kwakiutl way of life.

The Kwakiutl year is divided into two periods. Summer, *basux,* is the time for extensive hunting and fishing activities. The people live in small groups often separated by considerable distance. This is a time of limited ceremonial activity. During the winter, *tsetseqa,* the villages are occupied once again and this is the ceremonial time of the year. The Kwakiutl see these seasons almost as opposites, yet as interdependent. During the winter, the order of human existence is the reverse of the summer order. The people represent another form of being. They take winter names and corresponding appearances and actions to effect and express this reversal. Winter is the time for return to the

mythic era when human beings had animal forms and the people are organized into animal societies corresponding with varieties of spiritual or mythic
beings. The winter is actually not a time at all, in the sense of a succession of
new moments, but rather a reenactment of that timeless era of creation.

In the Kwakiutl view, the world corresponds with a total community of
four parts: human beings, animals, vegetable life, and supernatural beings. Each
of these categories has its own hierarchy and sets of antagonistic oppositions,
but the four are interdependent and interactive. In the mythic era, human
beings appeared in animal form, a mode of appearance conceived as human
beings wearing animal forms like removable masks. Thus, human beings and
animals were then identical. These humans appearing as animals were also
mythic personages and thereby gods. Upon creation, some of these beings
removed their animal forms to become the ancestors of human beings, while
others retained their animal forms as the ancestors of animal species.

Throughout the summer portion of the year, the relationship between
human beings and animals is that of hunter and hunted. The hunter kills and
eats the flesh of the animals. Eating of the animal flesh causes the animals to
become one with human beings but in human form. It is during the long,
elaborate Winter Ceremonial that this relationship is reversed. The primordial
identity of human and animal in animal form is enacted. Human beings take
up the masks of animals in ceremonial dances. By returning to the original
conditions they engender the supernatural powers of creation so as to benefit
the community.

Thus, a relationship of reciprocity lies beneath the interdependence of
human beings and animals. This reciprocity is completed by the role reversal
of hunter and game animal as the seasons change. In summer the animals
undergo death. In the winter, by means of the Winter Ceremonial, it is the
human beings who descend into darkness and death, thus restoring the animal
spirits. In this ceremonial process, human order must often pit its strengths
against supernatural antagonists who devour humans. This amounts to a
shamanic effort to recover the humans devoured by these deities. The pervasive use of cannibalistic and flesh-eating symbolism appropriately expresses
the Kwakiutl recognition of the basic interdependence of humans and animals. Also expressed in the Winter Ceremonial is the notion of the spiritual
counterpart to the physical world. Indeed, the very name for winter attests to
this. While the term *tsetseqa* was rendered by Franz Boas, as "fraudulent, pre-
tended, to cheat," Irving Goldman's recent analysis of the word indicates that
it more conveys the idea of imitation. This meaning corresponds with the
Kwakiutl concentration during this time on dramatic masked performances
by which they bring to presence, by imitation, the spiritual side of reality that
would otherwise remain hidden.

The central theme of the Winter Ceremonial, the devouring death and
resurgent life, is dramatically portrayed in the initiation rites of the *hamatsa*
society, part of which has been described. The initiate to this supernatural
order is the son of a member of the society. The rite by which he accepts his
inheritance to the society and the shamanic powers it possesses is also the way

in which he is introduced to the spiritual side of reality. The youth to be initiated is symbolically devoured by the Man Eater, an antagonistic deity who initially represents death. The Man Eater is depicted as having many mouths all over his body. He has an insatiable appetite for human flesh. He lives at the headwaters of the rivers at the north end of the world, a place of darkness, disease, and violent death. But the devourer is also a source of life, for one who has been devoured is transformed by his identity with the deity. If regurgitated and healed, he possesses new life invested with power.

After the youth is devoured, he is carried off to a remote corner of the forest, a place associated with the house of Man Eater. Here the youth undergoes a vision fast and learns the clan legend under the tutelage of members of the *hamatsa* society. This experience is equated to the metamorphosis of the youth who symbolically resides in the body of Man Eater. Under this influence, the youth becomes wild and develops a craving for human flesh. He takes a coffin from a tree (the Kwakiutl use this mortuary practice) and mimes eating the corpse. He must be reclaimed by the society as described.

This description of the initiation rites of the *hamatsa* society set against a background of the Kwakiutl way of life, illuminates the principles and beliefs that underlie the entire Winter Ceremonial as well as all of Kwakiutl religious thought. The Kwakiutl hold as vital the interrelationships between hunter and hunted, human and animal, human and spiritual, and summer and winter. Summer is the time when animals are hunted by human beings for the purpose of supplying food for ordinary human sustenance. During this time, animals and human beings appear as they ordinarily do in nature. This aspect of the relationship is reversed in winter, in a reciprocating process that completes their interdependence. Some human beings (the elders and initiated) ritually become animals and thereby represent spiritual beings as they reenter primordiality. The youth are given to antagonistic spirits to undergo ritual death by being devoured and in this way enter a chaotic state of madness. As in a shamanic initiation, the process of mortification and bodily reconstitution, symbolizing death and rebirth, invests one with great powers. Thus, the youth being initiated into the *hamatsa* society attains shamanic powers, the powers to communicate with the animals and the spiritual world. These powers accompany the rights and privileges of impersonating the animal forms in ceremonial dances.

In ceremonial dancing, the spirits are presented in their characteristic forms of movement. The masks and costumes portray their physical forms, and the songs reveal their nature. As in the mythic era, all are mythic figures who are human beings appearing in animal forms. To wear a mask is to participate in that reality.[10]

Much has been written about the well-known Kwakiutl and other Pacific Northwest Coast potlatches in which huge quantities of goods are given away. A study by Irving Goldman has reinterpreted this practice in terms that correct and surpass previous interpretations.[11] Popular views have often seen the potlatch as a spontaneous, angry exchange between ambitious rival chiefs, performed in a display of wealth intended to shame others and establish one's superior status. Goldman shows this view to be narrow and based on Western views of property, wealth, and rank. The potlatch may be better understood in the light of the Kwakiutl religious belief and way of life.

The goods exchanged in these ritual proceedings were traditionally animal skins. Blankets and other items have now replaced skins. To the Kwakiutl, animal skins are not merely dead currency, they are equivalent to the souls of the slain animals who, by giving up their lives, provide life for the people. The skin, by having visible form, is like a mask because it can be held and passed among members of the community. The animal skins or their equivalent, when ritually circulated among the societies whose work is to make present the mythic order of reality, are thereby participating in the process that is so important to Kwakiutl religion and life, that is, the mediation of the primordial world of human ancestors (animal people) and the ordinary world of hunter and hunted. It is through the ritual circulation of goods in which this quality of life is inherent that Kwakiutl reality is integrated and unified. In this way, the reciprocity that binds all interrelationships in the Kwakiutl world is complete.

There are many appropriate times for the potlatch giveaways, especially during the winter and on such occasions as marriage, when the demonstration of reciprocity is important. Potlatches are by no means confined to situations of antagonism; yet even when they are, they serve to complete the circulation of lives and life forces that integrates Kwakiutl religion and culture into an organic whole. The use of wealth in an antagonistic situation is part of the initiation into the *hamatsa* society. It was by feeding the maddened society and its tutelary, Man Eater, with human flesh, seawater (representing the wealth of the sea), and eagle down (representing the wealth of the air) that Man Eater gave up his hold on the youth and regurgitated him as a transformed powerful being. And it was by means of receiving goods associated with life that members of the *hamatsa* society became calm and effected a cure on the initiate.

Wealth stands for the vitality of the people in the Kwakiutl view. Through its circulation among the many, sometimes antagonistic, quarters of society, it is mediating, integrating, status-bestowing, and order-defining.

THE WINTUN HESI CEREMONY

The people native to the Sacramento Valley in northern California lived primarily on the wild fruits that grew abundantly there. Their chief mode of sustenance was gathering. They did not consider their abundance of food as simply a product of nature. Beliefs about the sources of food were intricately interwoven with their religious conception of the world. These beliefs required the frequent performance of ceremonial acts to assure the continuing abundance of wild harvest.

For the Wintun people who lived in this area, the most important of many annual ceremonials was known as Hesi. The date for this ceremonial was set by a shaman. During a trance, he or she would make a spiritual visit to the abode of the dead *(bole wilak)* to be instructed by the spiritual controller of the world *(katit)*. The shaman would not only be instructed about the date for the Hesi performance but also about the state of the world and human affairs.

The Hesi ceremonial, which lasted four days and nights, was conducted by the shaman in an earth-covered lodge that appeared as a swell in the landscape. The ceremonial was the occasion for numerous dances and lengthy ritual orations. Contents of these speeches included stories of the origin of the world as well as reports about progress toward the earth's final phase of history and the end of the world. A climactic moment during the ceremonial came when the shaman, serving also as director of the entire ceremonial, donned a ritual cloak to become a figure known as *moki*. The cloak was once a garment made of eagle feathers, but by the early part of the twentieth century it was made only of burlap strips. This cloaked figure entered the lodge and danced four times around the inside, constantly blowing a double whistle before stopping at the rear of the house to deliver a long speech spoken in a high-pitched, squeaky voice with the speaker bowing to the front and sides in gestures emphasizing various parts of the speech. *Moki*, while not a mythic figure, was recognized as a messenger from *katit*, keeper of the abode of the dead. The message from *katit* was mediated by the shaman appearing as *moki*. It instructed ways of proper conduct for the people and encouraged them to follow the Wintun way of life. The message made clear that the abundance of food was their reward for proper conduct and for following the instructions of *katit*. *Moki* functioned also to mediate to *katit* the needs of the people during the course of these ritual orations delivered in the earthen ceremonial lodge.[12]

THE ORIGINS OF CORN

The American origin of maize, commonly termed corn, and the great antiquity of corn cultivation in America are fundamental to the history of the cultures of North, Central, and South America. Corn was the most important and widely cultivated plant in the New World at the time of European contact. In North America it is grown in the eastern Plains, and especially the southeastern and southwestern United States.

Probably corn was first domesticated in southern Mexico. In the southern part of Puebla, Mexico, there is evidence of corn cultivation in the valley of Tehuacan dating to 4000 B.C.E. Corn was developed through the process of domestication from wild maize that grew throughout southern Mexico. Pollen of wild maize can be dated to 80,000 B.C.E. From its southern Mexican origin the development and diffusion of corn can be traced. Especially helpful in such tracing has been the identification of some 25 developed varieties of corn that can be separately accounted for. The oldest evidence of corn in North America is a variety of pod popcorn found in the area of Bat Cave, New Mexico. This corn is datable to 3000 B.C.E. and can be traced to origins in Mexico. The diffusion of corn cultivation, however, is not a simple story. Some strains can be traced from their origin in Mexico into the American Southwest, then to the Plains areas and on to the eastern United States. Other varieties moved from Mexico to South America through the West Indies to the southeastern United States and finally to the Southwest. Another diffusion pattern emerges from Mexico directly into the southeastern United States and upward along the Mississippi River and its tributaries.[13] Accompanying the gradual diffusion of corn cultivation and other agricultural influences, came changes in culture and religion.

Native American accounts of the origin of corn often attribute it to a goddess, a corn woman. In the southeastern United States, a Cherokee story accounts for the origin of both game and corn. Corn woman *(Selu)* is married to the master of game *(Konati)*. Their son finds a playmate, a boy who arose from blood that clotted when raw meat was washed in the river. The blood-clot boy is mischievous and entices his adopted brother into spying on their father when he goes to obtain meat. They observe him removing game from a cave or hole in the ground, its entrance guarded by a rock. After their father leaves, the boys investigate the spot. When they remove the stone, all of the game flee into the woods and remain fearful of human beings.

The boys also observe their mother producing food by rubbing her body. They believe this to be witchcraft and plot to kill their mother. Knowing their thoughts and her impending death at their hands, before her death she instructs them in the production of corn. She asks them to clear a piece of ground and drag her bleeding body seven times around over the field. When they do this, corn sprouts wherever the blood of the corn woman moistens the soil.[14]

This story shows the vital interrelationship between death and life, between the blood of death and blood as the source of life, a connection so obvious to hunting people undergoing transformation into an agricultural perspective. The blood becomes associated with feminine fertility, with waste and elimination, and with soil. The paradox of the identity of life and death is transformed and expanded into the paradox of the identity of waste (dirt, menstrual elimination, and epidermal waste) and food (corn and other cultivated plants). There is a shift from male domination in hunting cultures to female domination in agricultural cultures, from the sacrificial use of animals to that of humans or deities identified more with human than animal form. The Pawnee sacrifice to Morning Star has similar concerns.

The stories of the origin of corn take many forms, but they often accommodate other aspects of the way of life. Some Plains stories, for example, link the origin of corn with the origin of buffalo. The significance of corn is so profound and pervasive that for many Native American groups, especially in the southwestern Pueblo cultures, corn is synonymous with their worldviews and religions.[15]

This point can be illustrated by two specific examples. In the eastern United States, among the most common and frequently discussed ceremonial events are the green corn ceremonies, performed annually at the time of the corn harvest. An even richer example is seen in the way of life of the Tewa, an eastern Pueblo people in New Mexico.

THE GREEN CORN CEREMONIES
OF THE CREEK

The Creek, along with other cultures in the southeastern United States, were displaced to the Oklahoma territory during the 1830s in that tragic march known as the Trail of Tears. The green corn ceremonies so closely identified with the religions of the eastern and southeastern cultures doubtless underwent many changes, especially during the period of European contact, until their final performances in the late nineteenth century. Some residual performances persisted after the move to Oklahoma. As a result, the accounts of the green corn ceremonies arise from a variety of sources including literate Native Americans, travelers, traders, and ethnographers. These accounts range over a considerable period of time.[16]

The well-known Creek green corn ceremonial is often identified by the term busk derived from the Creek *posketa,* which means fast. The ceremonial occurred in July or August in correspondence with the ripening of the corn. It was performed just when the green corn is at the stage of turning color. Normally the ceremonial lasted four days, but at least one detailed account describes an eight-day event. The activities centered on a square specially prepared ceremonial ground located some distance from the village or town. Low sheds of log construction were arranged, one on each side of the square and open only on the inside. These housed the various orders of performers. In preparation for the ceremonial, the residences (especially the hearths) were cleaned, friendships were repaired, and trespasses (even crimes, except for the gravest) were forgiven. All fires were extinguished. Four logs, each a couple of yards in length, were cut and placed in the center of the ceremonial ground and oriented to the cardinal directions. In the center, a new fire was ignited by use of a fire drill. Upon this fire the medicine decoctions were prepared and the men, who confined themselves for four days primarily to the ceremonial ground area, entered a period of fasting, frequently drinking an emetic to aid in their purgation. Food taboos were extended to the whole community. Especially forbidden was the eating of the new corn before the conclusion of the ceremonial. The eating of salt was also forbidden and relations between the men and women were restricted.

The new fire was known as breath master and the medicine men would blow through a tube into the infusion of medicines they prepared on the new fire. Offerings were made to the fire of green corn and other items, including a black drink prepared from roasted green corn. Later the women were permitted to come to the ceremonial grounds to receive the new fire for use on their own hearths. During the first three days the men fasted and purged themselves while dancing was done by select groups of men, women, or both.

On the last day, the fast was broken and the new foods could then be eaten. This was a day of dancing and mock battles.

Green corn ceremonialism shows that the ripening of corn was perceived as the dominant feature in the institution of a new year. It was the focus around which life was not only possible but also made meaningful. The busk was a time of peace and forgiveness, of communion and renewal. It was a time of repair, cleaning, and fresh beginnings. It was a time for celebrating the forthcoming bounty of life in the initiation of a new world. It was also a time for religious renewal and communion with the spiritual world. It invoked order and served to originate a new time.

THE TEWA WAY OF LIFE

For the Tewa, as for other Pueblo people in the American Southwest, corn is both the primary subsistence and the most potent religious symbol. Aspects of the complex religious systems of the Hopi, Zuni, and Cochiti have already been described. These are complemented by a consideration of the Tewa as recounted by Tewa anthropologist Alfonso Ortiz.[17]

Fundamental to the Tewa annual pattern is the clear distinction made between winter and summer. This is reflected in the social structure that has the summer-winter moiety division. The entire Tewa society is divided into two groups, identified respectively with winter and summer. This distinction was defined at the creation of the Tewa in the primordial underworld known as *Sipofene,* which is located beneath a lake north of the present Tewa residence. At that time, deities, humans, and animals lived together along with the first mothers of the Tewa—Blue Corn Woman, the summer mother, and White Corn Maiden, the winter mother. From these primal mothers originated the winter and summer moieties. Summer is the time for planting and harvesting corn and other cultivated crops. Winter is the time for nonagricultural activities, especially hunting. Summer is ruled by the chief of the summer moiety, winter by the winter chief.

This dual system seems simple enough, but the Tewa way of life is not simply an oscillation between winter and summer. In the Tewa view, successful progress through the annual and life cycles requires a more complicated structure that effects movement from moment to moment, the transitions from season to season. This structure is based on a process that unifies the natural and material world of the Tewa with the supernatural and spiritual levels of Tewa reality. It is this ordering of the way of life that gives it unity and meaning.

According to Ortiz, the Tewa classify all existence into three pairs of linked categories. One aspect or member of each pair is material or natural. In Tewa terms, this single aspect is *seh t'a,* which refers to all existence after emergence generally as hardened matter—or literally, dry food. The other member of each pair is spiritual, either that which never emerged, that is, the principal deities who remained below the earth surface after the people and animals emerged, or those souls of human beings who, after death, returned to the spiritual domain below the earth surface. The categories are these: Dry Food People and their spiritual counterpart consisting of the souls of their dead, known as Dry Food People Who Are No Longer; Towa é and their spiritual counterpart, known also as Towa é; and Made People and their spiritual counterpart Dry Food Who Never Did Become, that is, those deities who never emerged.

The Towa é pair serves primarily to mediate between the other linked pairs. In the human sphere, this pair consists of the elected political officials representing both moieties. The Dry Food People are common Tewa people. The Made People are adult Tewa who enter any of eight groups whose primary business it is to mediate between the material/natural world and the spiritual/supernatural world. Their efforts assure orderly progress through the annual cycle and thereby assure life for the Tewa people. Generally each of these groups is composed of people from both moieties, and both genders.

The Made People are the religious and social elite of the Tewa, for they control all human activities. Their primary responsibility is to assure the continuity of the processes of life. Throughout the year, the Made People have nine specified periods of activity, called works by Ortiz. These are associated with phases in a sequence that must be followed in the Tewa life way. Each of these works engages each of the eight groups of Made People in a prayerful retreat. These retreats last a day and a night, during which the members of the society offer prayers and perform rites to insure that the seasonal changes take place. Each group performs its work separately at four-day intervals, so there is constant activity by the Made People for thirty-two days during each of these nine works.

The works of the Made People effectively create the passage of time for the Tewa. It is in these works that the Tewa world is made to correspond with the paradigm or model established at creation, and through these works the natural and supernatural worlds are kept in contact. The human world and Tewa way of life are wholly dependent on the spiritual world, which never did become. While these works of the Made People engage both moieties, the works still reflect the basic winter–summer distinction. For example, the work performed in February, which begins just after the Winter Chief transfers responsibility to the Summer Chief, is known as "bringing the buds to life." The March work is called "bringing the leaves to life." Those in August and September are concerned with harvest. The works of the winter are not concerned with agriculture.

When correlated with the annual ritual or ceremonial cycle these works of the Made People are the basis for the entire Tewa life way. All public ritual activity throughout the annual cycle is planned and directed by the Made People. Each of the eight groups of Made People is responsible for at least one major public ritual. Some of these are accomplished by the Made People themselves in masked performances of the deities who are their spiritual counterparts, Made People Who Never Did Become. Other rituals are performed by the Dry Food People under the administration of the Towa é. In every case, the performance of ritual depends on successful completion of the works of the Made People. The ritual cycle reflects the distinction between winter and summer activities and serves to mediate through public performances the effects achieved by the works of the whole Tewa community. What the Made People accomplish privately now becomes public through these ritual activities.

While all of these works and rituals assure the successful life of the Tewa people, they do not accomplish the banal planting, harvesting, and hunting activities. These daily activities correlate with the works and rituals, they correspond with and follow from them. Such ordinary activities proceed only according to this religious mediation and effective action, thus assuring their proper and successful performance. In these mundane sustenance activities is reflected the distinction between summer and winter activities.

At the base of the Tewa worldview is a duality, expressed as winter-summer and material/natural-spiritual/supernatural. This duality is unified and mediated principally by the Tewa system of classifying all existence in terms of three pairs of linked categories. Each of these pairs in itself bridges the material-spiritual duality, and the pairs taken together form a hierarchy that mediates and thereby integrates the winter-summer division, which exists in both the material and spiritual worlds. The entire Tewa way of life proceeds on the life-giving dynamics of this organization.

Ortiz's work also shows that this same ordering that corresponds with the winter-summer annual cycle is replicated in the Tewa landscape, which is bound at its outermost limits by four mountains, one in each of the cardinal directions. Each of these mountains is associated with a lake or pond beneath each of which is a group residence of the Dry Food People Who Never Did Become. Each mountain and corresponding lake is associated with an appropriate directional color. At the top of each mountain is an earth navel, associated with the spiritual Towa é. Closer to the Tewa village in each cardinal direction are four flat-topped hills. Each hill has a cave or labyrinth and is the residence of the spirit figures who are impersonated by the human Towa é in ritual. Still closer to the village in each of the cardinal directions stands a major shrine. This is the residence of the souls of all things that have lived. A final notable set of features approaching the center of the Tewa landscape are the four pueblos or Tewa houses that surround the four dance plazas.

The set of three pairs of linked categories are thus represented by correspondence with these distinctive features in the Tewa landscape. The spiritual/supernatural aspect of each pair corresponds with the outer realms, that is, with the mountains, lakes, hills, and shrines. The corresponding material/natural members of these pairs are represented in the human domain of the pueblos, dance plazas, and divisions in the social structure of the Tewa people.

Further, the winter-summer moiety division is represented in the landscape, for the north and east are associated with winter, while the south and west are associated with summer. Even the spiritual figures associated with the lakes, mountains, hills, and shrines are grouped within each level of the spiritual hierarchy by their associations with winter and summer. This is represented in the impersonation of these figures, by ritual attire, dances, and manners that identify them with the direction and season to which they belong.

Notably in this geographic or spatial scheme there is no simple opposition between spiritual and material, between other-than-human and human. For example, the earth navels at the extremities of the Tewa landscape mark the dwelling places of the most important beings, the Dry Food People Who Never Did Become who are as religiously valued as is the "Earth mother earth navel middle place" located in the center of the village.

This description of the Tewa religious system is complicated, but it only hints at the sophistication of the Tewa worldview. Beyond suggesting the impressiveness of Tewa religious thought it shows that, on the one hand, the Tewa make· extensive and rigid classifications while, on the other, the interactions of these classifications achieve a dynamic, vital unity that defines a way of life. This way of life is richly meaningful at many different levels in many different ways. Most significant is that the basis for this complex system is a religious conception of the world, attested by the fundamental truths of the creation stories, by the constant enactment of ritual activities, and by the orientation within a complexly significant landscape.

CONCLUSION

For Native Americans, sustenance and sustenance activities are an important means of articulating religious worldview and enacting religious value. As such, most ordinary activities related to food are accompanied by or synonymous with ritual activity and religious ideas. Native Americans live their religion through their sustaining ways of life.

NOTES

1. Alfred Kroeber, "World Renewal: A Cult System of Native Northwest California," *University of California Anthropological Records,* vol. 13, no. 1 (1949).

2. A. Irving Hallowell, "Bear Ceremonialism in the Northern Hemisphere," *American Anthropologist* 28(1926):1–175.

3. Alanson Skinner, *Notes on the Eastern Cree and Northern Saulteaux,* Anthropological Papers, vol. 9, part 1 (New York: American Museum of Natural History, 1911), p. 162.

4. See Ibid., pp. 68–76, 162–64.

5. A. Irving Hallowell, "Ojibwa Ontology, Behavior, and World View," in *Culture in History: Essays in Honor of Paul Radin,* ed. Stanley Diamond (New York: Columbia University Press, 1960), pp. 19–52.

6. Ibid., p. 24.

7. See Richard M. Dorson, *Bloodstoppers and Bearwalkers* (Cambridge: Harvard University Press, 1952).

8. Margaret Lantis, *Alaskan Eskimo Ceremonialism,* Monographs of the American Ethnological Society, no. 11 (Seattle: University of Washington Press, 1947).

9. This description is based on Werner Muller, "North America," in *Pre-Columbian American Religions,* ed. Walter Krickeberg (London: Weidenfeld and Nicolson, 1968), pp. 209–20; and Irving Goldman, *The Mouth of Heaven: An Introduction to Kwakiutl Religious Thought* (New York: John Wiley, 1975), pp. 86–97.

10. See Goldman, *The Mouth of Heaven,* pp. 86–121, for a discussion of the Winter Ceremonial.

11. See Ibid., pp. 122–76.

12. S. A. Barrett, "The Wintun Hesi Ceremony," *University of California Publications in American Archaeology and Ethnology,* vol. 14, no. 4 (Berkeley: University of California Press, 1919), pp. 438–88.

13. See Harold E. Driver, *Indians of North America,* rev. ed. (Chicago: University of Chicago Press, 1969), pp. 66–70, Map 7.

14. James Mooney, *Myths of the Cherokee,* Smithsonian Institution, Bureau of American Ethnology, 19th Annual Report (Washington, D.C., 1900), pp. 242–49; and James Mooney, "Myths of the Cherokee," *Journal of American Folklore* 1 (1888): 98–106.

15. See Gudmund Hatt, "The Corn Mother in America and in Indonesia," *Anthropos* 46 (1951): 853–911.

16. John Witthoft, *Green Corn Ceremonialism in the Eastern Woodlands,* Occasional Contributions from the Museum of Anthropology of the University of Michigan (Ann Arbor, 1949); see especially the section on Creek, pp. 52–70.

17. Alfonso Ortiz, *The Tewa World: Space, Time, Being and Becoming in a Pueblo Society* (Chicago: University of Chicago Press, 1969).

7

ﬔ

Tradition and Change
in Native American
Religions

Among the most beautiful Navajo poems are the horse songs.

Its feet are made of mirage.
Its gait was a rainbow.
Its bridle of sun strings.
Its heart was made of red stone.
Its intestines were made of water of all kinds.
Its tail of black rain.
Its mane was a cloud with a little rain.
Distant lightning composed its ears.
A big spreading twinkling star formed its eye and striped its face.
Its lower legs were white.
At night beads formed its lips.
White shell formed its teeth.
A black flute was put into its mouth for a trumpet.
Its belly was made of dawn, one side white, one side black.[1]

The horse is described in the song to correspond with the shape of the Navajo world. The history and present status of the Navajo people have been deeply influenced by the horse. Even though pickup trucks have now replaced the horse for transportation, horses are still kept by many Navajo families as an expression of their wealth and status. The pickup truck can also be seen as an extension of the horse in the sense that it provides a means of movement by which the people may continue their way of life—a way defined by that paradox of choosing to occupy vast regions of land while restlessly, even aggressively, seeking mastery over distance.

In historical perspective the horse, now an image of cosmic proportion for the Navajo, was introduced to North America by the Spanish only four centuries ago. This raises fundamental questions not only with regard to the Navajo but to the consideration of Native American religions. For this image, which we recognize as traditional for Navajos, is actually a product of the same European influences often identified as threatening the existence of Native American cultures.

The most traditional, typical, and distinctive features of Native American religions are commonly entwined with their histories including elements of outside influence originating both in Europe and in other native cultures. Native American traditions must be also understood in light of their histories. Every aspect of Native American religions has a place in a long, complex history, and every form of expression and religious act is part of a history. While it has been impractical to give more than occasional reminders of this fact in previous chapters, these historical processes are the focus in this chapter because they are as important and distinctive as any other dimension of Native American religions.

Persistent colonial efforts have long been directed to suppress, alter, and eliminate Native American traditions. Yet many of these traditions have survived by a skillful management of historical events that has permitted Native American people to protect and strengthen their traditions as well as to adapt them to the changes forced on them. In light of the actual survival of these traditions under such oppressive conditions, it is clear that historical processes are among the most distinctively important aspects of Native American religious traditions.

History, in the technical sense, denotes a written record or account of the past, a narrative in which meaning is constructed through the presentation of temporally causal sequences. For Native Americans, until recently, this sort of narrative did not exist. What is the constant concern however, that it be considered history, is the developmental sequence, the creative management of change, the acknowledgment that tradition implies a meaningful interconnection and ongoing sequence of change.

The history of Native American religions is complex and difficult to piece together because of the short span of recorded history. Even in the historical period, which is coincident with the period of European contact, there has been little concern with recording the religious histories of native cultures. What written histories that do exist, usually focus on European interests in native cultures. Thus, the known and recorded history of Native American religions is linked directly to the eradication of native traditions and to their Christianization.

RIO GRANDE PUEBLOS

From a tourist turnout on Interstate 40 west of Albuquerque, New Mexico, one can see the Pueblo village of Laguna. The houses of the village span the southeast side of a small hill. Pueblo houses dot the hillside, but the sight is dominated by the Catholic church that stands near the hilltop, easily identifiable by its massive size in contrast to the small houses and by its cross-topped steeple.

One early spring morning, I observed Laguna from a different perspective. I ventured off the highway and drove into the village. Even from this perspective, the Catholic church was dominant, for the people from the village were making their way to the church for the celebration of mass. It was a minor fiesta day in Laguna, a gala event with concession stands selling food and numerous visitors from other pueblos arriving throughout the morning. In the afternoon of this chilly, windy day, I went to the village plaza to watch the Laguna dances, but the plaza was deserted. As I awaited the appearance of the dancers, I began to hear the beat of drums, the shake of rattles, and voices singing the Laguna songs. The sounds carried on the wind led me to the Catholic church, where I watched the Laguna dancing. The dancers, both men and women, wore European-American clothing, but some wore moccasins and others wore brightly colored scarves as headbands. All carried rattles as two parallel files performed the dance steps. The priest of the church in his rope-sashed brown robe appeared at the front apparently performing ordinary custodial duties. He seemed to pay little attention to the Pueblo activities that occupied the church.[2]

From the door at the rear of the church, I looked past the dancers to view the Christian symbols—the altar, crucifix, stations of the cross—but some architectural features, numerous designs painted on the beams, and other items were distinctively Puebloan. I thought of the Catholic mission church at the Pueblo village of Zuni, where larger-than-life paintings of *koko (kachina)* figures dominate the walls. I thought of the numerous Pueblo villages that cluster along the Rio Grande River, villages in which the mission church is the dominant building. I thought of the large dance plazas adjacent to these churches, where Pueblo dances, highly religious in character, are frequently performed. These observations of common features reflect certain peculiar anomalies as witness to the present moment in a long and remarkable religious history. It is a history in which Christian and native religions have been in almost continuous contact for 400 years. The first Franciscan missionaries began establishing themselves among the Pueblo people nearly 40 years before the Mayflower sailed in 1620. The city of Santa Fe, which lies amidst the Rio Grande Pueblo area, became the provincial capital of New Mexico in 1610.

Most remarkable is that after this long history, the Pueblo people have maintained their native religious tradition and way of life. Indeed, the Pueblo people are closely associates with the idea of an ancient, strongly indigenous tradition.

Yet it is nonetheless obvious that the Pueblo people (the Hopi far to the west somewhat excepted) have also accepted Christianity and incorporated it into their Pueblo way of life. The tenacity, adaptability, and ability to compartmentalize are all characteristics of Pueblo religious historical processes, which cannot be understood or appreciated apart from at least an outline of Pueblo religious and cultural history.[3]

Based on linguistic and archaeological data and the projections that can be made from the ethnographic record, the outlines of the prehistoric period that preceded Coronado's entrance into the Rio Grande area in 1540 can be sketched. The people who lived in the area during this time can definitely be identified as comprising two distinct traditions that had entered the area at different times. Probably first to enter were the Tanoans, believed to have come from what is now the northeastern corner of Arizona and the northwestern corner of New Mexico. They came from the areas known today as Anasazi, Mesa Verde, and Chaco, probably entering the Rio Grande area between 1100 and 1200. They were followed by the Keresan people, believed to have come from the area of today's east-central Arizona. Their descendants have remained linguistically distinct, and they continue to bear basic cultural differences.

During this early period, these groups established themselves in settlements along the Rio Grande River and its tributaries and turned to an agricultural subsistence pattern adapted to the ready water supply from the river. Their former agricultural methods had depended more on rainfall, but in this new environment they could use irrigation. Close community organization was necessary to build and maintain the irrigation system.

There is evidence that contact among these two traditions was widespread during this prehistoric period, but it is likely that these cultures also had much contact with other cultures. Certainly there was contact with the Apachean people who were entering the area from their former homelands in distant western Canada. There is also evidence of widespread contact with the Plains cultures who, at this time, were sedentary agriculturalists. Thus, during the several centuries before the initial European contact, the people living in the Rio Grande valley experienced frequent cultural interaction accompanied by borrowing and cultural innovation.

The Pueblo ceremonial system was well developed and, while there were basic differences in approach and emphasis, the Tanoan and Keresan traditions focused on controlling weather, curing the ill, and maintaining good health, warfare, and controlling game animals and fowl. The Tanoan approach emphasized works, in the manner of the Tewa, while the Keresan approach emphasized magical practices to accomplish these concerns.

History, in its written form, began for the Rio Grande Pueblo people in 1540 with the appearance of Coronado, who was accompanied by five missionaries, several hundred armed horsemen, and a group of native servants from Mexico. The first encounter was not a happy one for the Pueblo people, for Coronado demanded much from them during his two-year stay in the area. Attempts to protest were answered by executions numbering in the hundreds.

Second and third Spanish expeditions followed some 40 years later. The second was short, but two missionaries were left behind, and it is believed that they were soon killed by the Pueblos. The third expedition, led by Espejo in 1582, inspired much interest in colonization of the area. In 1598, Juan de Oñate established the first colony in the province of New Mexico near San Juan. During the next century, the Pueblo people were constantly confronted by a demanding Spanish presence. The major arenas of contact were in the Pueblo villages, with the intrusive establishment of Franciscan missions, and in the Spanish settlements, where Pueblo people were forced to work for the colonial governors and settlers.

The missionary attitudes toward the indigenous people is important. Franciscan policy frequently rotated their missionaries from station to station and back and forth between Mexico and these northern posts. Consequently the Franciscans took little interest in making enduring associations with the Pueblo people. With rare exception, the missionaries did not learn their languages, engage in translating Christian scripture or beliefs into their languages, or adapt their efforts to suit Pueblo cultures. Instead they primarily exerted themselves to accomplish several goals, each of which they approached in a manner that bred only antagonism and distrust between themselves and the native people.

A major concern of the missionaries, still in evidence, was an enormous building program. Large chapels and mission compounds were built in the villages accomplished by forced Pueblo labor. The size of these buildings testifies to the measure of labor that was invested. The huge timbers that supported their roofs often had to be cut and hauled by the Pueblo workers from a distance of 20 to 30 miles. By 1630, it was reported that 90 chapels existed in as many villages. The missionaries introduced Christianity in a manner similar to the way they built their chapels. Under punishment of whipping, they forced the native people to be baptized, to attend mass, and to make confession. They physically discouraged the performance of native religious practices. Many were the occasions when native religious leaders were hanged as witches and when *kivas* (religious chambers) were raided for the ceremonial paraphernalia and masks, which were collected and burned. Missionaries, like the colonists, also forced the native people to tend their gardens and domestic animals and to perform other personal services. The effect was to force the practice of Pueblo religion underground, to introduce a participation in Christian acts but with little internalized meaning, and to breed a deep resentment of the Spanish and the Christian church.

The colonial arena of contact was no more pleasant. It was a period of encroachment on Pueblo lands. While enslavement was illegal, a system of *encomienda* was established that gave colonists control of the native people on the land granted to them. This permitted colonists to force the Pueblo people to work for them without compensation.

The supremacy of the Spanish, fully realized by the Pueblo people, fostered a resurgence of loyalty and dedication to traditional ways. This resurgence of identity, encouraged by ever-increasing bewilderment and resentment, set the scene for a Pueblo revolt throughout the area in 1680. Carefully planned by a Pueblo man from San Juan by the name of Popé, who had been one of 47 religious leaders punished by the Spanish authorities in 1675, the revolt effectively removed the Spanish from the entire Rio Grande area. Twenty-one of 33 missionaries and nearly 400 of 2,500 colonists were killed, the rest fled to the El Paso area. The missions were destroyed together with all their records and furnishings and the Pueblo people lived free of Spanish influence until De Varga arrived to reconquer the area in 1693. At this time, many Pueblo people fled from the area to live among the Pueblo people to the west and even among non-Pueblo people like the Navajo and Apache. The village of Laguna was founded to the west of the Rio Grande in an attempt to avoid Spanish domination. During the seventeenth century, epidemics, violent deaths, and dispersal had greatly declined the Rio Grande Pueblo population.

The extensive changes that occurred during the seventeenth century were surprising in character. While not forced to do so, the Pueblo people effected a wide range of changes in their culture. By 1700 they had added wheat, melons, apples, peaches, apricots, pears, tomatoes, and chiles to their crops. They had acquired chickens, goats, and sheep as domestic animals, adding not only to their diet but introducing craft items made from wool. They had begun to use mules, horses, and donkeys for transportation and for assistance with their labor. These additions revolutionized their cultures and have been so totally incorporated that they are now an integral part of the traditional ways of these cultures.

But while the Catholic chapels had by this time come to dominate the village architecture, the Catholic missions apparently had little effect on the Pueblo religious beliefs and practices, apart from forcing into secrecy performance of the native tradition and forcing the tacit public performance of Christian acts. More extensive effects on Pueblo religion resulted from contact with the native people brought from Mexico and increased contact among native people in the Rio Grande area.

During the seventeenth century, Spanish had become a second language, providing a lingua franca among the many native people whose languages were unintelligible to one another, yet they retained their own languages and even made efforts to keep them free of Spanish words. Because the Spanish language permitted them to better communicate among themselves, it became an instrument used by the Pueblo people against Spanish intrusions. It helped support the growing sense of unity and common identity that replaced the antagonisms that existed prior to Spanish contact.

While the eighteenth and nineteenth centuries also witnessed strong external influence in the Rio Grande area, it was, in many respects, less threatening to the Pueblo people than the influence that had occurred before. Spanish attitudes and policies changed after reconquest to emphasize colonization, and efforts to Christianize the Pueblos were relaxed. As colonization progressed, the frequent raids by non-Pueblo native people harassed colonists and Pueblo people alike and they joined together in an effort to combat these threats. The influx of colonists provided another major charge for the Franciscan missionaries in serving these growing communities.

The eighteenth-century relations between Pueblo and Spanish people was generally friendly, both parties being occupied with maintaining their own ways and identities. The remaining thorn for the Pueblo people was the Spanish clergy, who continued, though with less vigor, to force Pueblo participation in the Catholic missions and to infringe upon them for labor and other services. During this century, the Pueblo people apparently perfected ways of accommodating the demands of the Spanish and especially the missionaries by yielding to the performance of certain acts with little or no commitment or internalization of their European meanings, while retrenching and deepening their commitment to their own traditions. When borrowing did occur, it was usually accomplished in direct continuity with the Pueblo tradition.

The nineteenth century saw the appearance of Anglo-Americans and the U.S. government in the area. The largest cultural group was Hispanic, and because these people were most concerned with continuing to establish themselves in the area, they had little interest in changing Pueblo life. New Mexico became a U.S. territory in 1850, however, and this new government influence only added to the confusion about land rights among the several people in the area. This period was most difficult for the Pueblo people because their legal status with respect to their ownership of lands was in general dispute. By 1881, railroads had penetrated the area, and with them came a new economic base for the Pueblo people. A flood of tourists who were curious about Indians began to wash over the area. Their eagerness to buy from the Native Americans contributed to the introduction of a cash economy to the Pueblos. In one report from this period, a Pueblo woman expressed how odd these Americans were, for one of them had bought the stone that covered her chimney.

Despite all of the innovations accepted in terms of material culture by 1700, the traditions of the Pueblo people had remained firm through the two following centuries. The village locations, social order, value system, and ceremonial system had remained in good health. The Pueblos had continued to be tightly integrated, self-sustaining communities living full ceremonial lives. By 1900, several of the mission churches had fallen into ruin, but the Pueblo religious tradition continued to be vigorously practiced, now under the veil of intense secrecy.

With the rapid rise of the Anglo-American influence in New Mexico, the first half of the twentieth century was a period when changes occurred on an order far more profound than the Pueblos had undergone in the previous three centuries of contact. Prior to the Anglo-American dominance, the Pueblo cultures had been challenged largely by the Spanish Catholic missionaries who had attempted to destroy the traditional Pueblo religion and introduce Christianity. This effort backfired and resulted in a deeply entrenched Pueblo religious tradition protected by the range of isolating protective mechanisms that had been carefully developed over centuries. Yet, the Pueblo people had readily accepted innovations in material culture and had established them firmly in continuity with their traditions. These innovations were of a type that supported the closely integrated, separate identity of each Pueblo community.

But with the Anglo-American dominance came basic economic changes: the introduction of the credit system by establishing trading posts and the expansion of a cash economy. These economic conditions fostered sweeping changes in the character of Pueblo society. In the 1930s, the U.S. Bureau of Indian Affairs engaged in a construction program aimed at bringing Native Americans into fuller participation in a complex U. S. economy. This tendency was further expanded during World War II. Not only were many Pueblo people engaged in the armed services, but jobs could be easily obtained outside the Pueblo villages. This broad-scale participation in a complex cash economy, once accepted, has continued to expand. Today, most Pueblo communities continue to farm and maintain some semblance of a subsistence-type economy, but this is almost a token effort. Most Pueblos depend on wage and salary incomes from outside the community, often in major urban centers. This has engaged the Pueblo people not only in broader interaction and interdependence with non-Pueblo people, it has also introduced to them the importance of a pan-cultural identity. They have come to interact and identify more completely with other native people, a development evidenced by their participation in numerous intertribal affairs and also in the activities of major urban centers that contain a significant Native American population.

The ceremonial system and the practice of traditional Pueblo religion have undergone and survived their greatest challenges during this period. The official position of the Bureau of Indian Affairs before 1928 was openly antagonistic toward Indian ceremonials. It outlawed them and made every effort to discourage the continuity of such traditions, attempting to bring the Pueblo communities into complete assimilation with the Anglo-American majority culture. The Pueblo people had well-developed and well-practiced mechanisms to meet this challenge and to renew dedication to their religious traditions. These methods helped encourage a unified resistance among the members of the Pueblo communities.

When John Collier became head of the Bureau of Indian Affairs he soon changed this position. He respected the traditions of Native Americans and supported the practice of their ceremonials. He encouraged programs to support the survival of Native American communities by helping to establish them in the vital areas of economy, education, and health services.

The result was a series of developments that have greatly transformed the Pueblo communities since the beginning of the seventeenth century. Today, while most Pueblo villages have survived, the compact village structure has given way to isolated single-family dwellings, often built in new settlement areas. These houses are patterned on American suburban homes with garages, lawns, electricity, plumbing, and all of the furnishings one would find in the average Anglo-American home. Cars and pickup trucks are essential in connecting the communities with job locations and with the external sources of food and other items purchased on credit or for cash. Television has replaced, to a major extent, the sessions of storytelling. Dress and hair styles are largely Anglo, yet still serve to indicate the degree to which a person is traditional or progressive. English has become the second language, replacing Spanish, and with each generation English is increasingly becoming the primary, often the only, language known.

Broadening of the Pueblo subsistence and economic base has brought greater possibility for the people to internalize the traditional meanings of Christianity and to recognize that it serves the same general needs as the traditional Pueblo religious practices, the health and well-being of all humanity. Still, the ceremonial organization and practice of traditional religions have been retained to a remarkable degree, though finding sufficient numbers of people to fill the necessary societies and religious offices has become increasingly difficult for many villages. In this area of culture, however, lies the future continuity of identity and tradition for the Pueblo communities.

On fiesta day in Laguna, what I observed was the present phase in a long and complex religious history. Against the outline of this history, the separateness of the Catholic and native practices is unclear, yet the genuine meaningfulness of both these forms of religious practice for contemporary Pueblo people is as well. While the separate performance attests to the remarkable persistence and self-preservation of the Pueblo traditions, the voluntary participation in Christian practices and the adjustment of native practices to correlate with the Christian liturgical calendar attests to the present most remarkable stage in Pueblo religious history. It indicates the extent to which Pueblo people can extend their ideas about religion to encompass even the Christian beliefs they have carefully isolated for centuries in their continuing efforts to meet the new needs of their rapidly changing cultures.

YAQUI

On the south side of the Phoenix area, just three miles from where I used to live, is the Yaqui community of Guadalupe. For many years during Easter week, I went to Guadalupe to observe the celebration of their highest religious occasion. The Yaqui church at Guadalupe stands beside the Spanish Catholic church, facing east and overlooking a large plaza area. During Easter week, this plaza area is remarkably transformed. On the side in front of the Spanish Catholic church, a carnival is set up complete with ferris wheel, tilt-a-whirl, merry-go-round, and game booths with their barkers. In front of the Yaqui church, the plaza area is roped off and reserved for the dramatic ritual performances of the Easter pageantry. This area is surrounded by temporary stands, erected by the Yaqui people, in which they prepare and sell a variety of food and craft items to the many people who come to observe the events.

The Easter Festival engages the Yaqui community throughout the period of Lent, but many in the community are totally immersed in the dramatic activities that unfold during Holy Week. At this time, the story of the crucifixion and resurrection of Jesus is enacted to ritually dramatize the basic struggle between good and evil. These forces are presented by groups or societies of Yaqui performers.

The Fariseo society is in charge of the Easter ceremonies. In the Easter pageant, this society provides several groups of performers. The Soldiers of Rome are a small group whose members wear ordinary dress but serve as officers to the other Fariseo performers. It is their responsibility to direct the fiesta and they must remember every detail of the extensive performance.

The Pilatos, who represent Pontius Pilate, are the ritual heads of the Fariseo society. They wear black shirts and wide-brimmed hats, and they carry spears. The largest group of Fariseos are the Chapayekas, who are masked figures. Several types of masks may be worn, but the most characteristic is distinctive for its big flat ears and sharp nose. Indeed, the word Chapayeka is derived from Yaqui words meaning sharp and nose. These masks may serve as caricatures of all sorts of figures associated with evil. The Chapayeka performer always carries the cross of his rosary in his mouth to protect him from the evil he serves to manifest. Chapayekas wear an overcoat or a blanket wrapped around them like a coat with a belt of rattles. They also carry a wooden sword and dagger.

Another group, not a part of the Fariseo society but associated with them in the Passion performance, is the Caballeros. They march with the Fariseos and try to keep the Chapayekas from going too far in their threatening antics.

On the side opposing the Fariseos is the society of the Matachinis. This society presides over all other ceremonials performed during the year. As a group of male dancers, they appear wearing no special costume other than a headdress made of crepe paper strips wrapped around a bamboo frame. They carry a brightly colored gourd in one hand and a brightly colored feather wand in the other. Several other groups also perform during the Easter pageant: the Maestros (teachers), who read the services and serve as church officials; the Cantoras, women who sing the chants in the choir; and several others that perform custodial activities throughout the performance.

Some performances during the Easter Festival have origins which precede Christian influences. The Pascola (old man of the fiesta) dances to the alternate accompaniment of the drum and flute, and the harp and violin. He wears a cotton blanket sashed with a belt of sleighbells around his hips. Barefooted, he wears cocoon rattles around his ankles. He carries a rattle that he sounds by beating it against his open palm. His long hair is tied with a red ribbon, and he wears a black wooden mask decorated with white designs. The performance of the Deer Dancer is also well known at this time. The Deer Dancer wears a dark-colored shawl around his hips over pants rolled up almost to the knees. He wears cocoon rattles on his ankles and a deer-hoof rattle belt. On his head over a white cloth is a deer head, worn during the dance performance. The Deer

Dancer performs to the accompaniment of percussion music made by scraper rasps and a half-gourd, beaten while held in a pan of water which serves as a resonator.

Throughout Lent the forces of evil slowly engender more and more power. This rising threat is dramatically portrayed on such occasions as the Friday evening services when the community celebrates the Way of the Cross following a path of several city blocks around the village area immediately surrounding the church and plaza. By Holy Week the presence of evil has become so strong that it begins assaulting the church in an effort to take control of it. On Wednesday (Tenebrae), the Fariseos begin their search for Jesus. On Thursday, they chase Viejito, an old man who is like Jesus. They taunt and make fun of him but do not kill him, for he is old. They continue to search for Jesus and finally find him (a sculpted representation) in a cottonwood bower, which has been constructed to represent the Garden of Gethsemane. They destroy the bower and capture the figure of Jesus, taking him to the church, where he is held captive while the Chapayekas stand guard over him all night. In control of the church with Jesus as their captive, the forces of evil seem to have triumphed. There is apparent confirmation of this on Good Friday, when Jesus is crucified and entombed.

But the triumph of evil is short, for in the predawn hours of Saturday morning, the Fariseos discover that Jesus has risen. With the resurrection, the forces of good slowly begin to reassert themselves. A new fire ceremony is celebrated. Later a straw figure of Judas, the betrayer of Jesus dressed like a Chapayeka, is borne by the Chapayekas on the back of a burro around the Way of the Cross but in the wrong direction. Judas is fastened to a cross in the plaza. The Chapayekas dance before this figure thus honoring their chief. Sensing their loss of power, the Fariseos repeatedly launch attacks upon the church, but they are repelled by flowers and confetti thrown at them. Flowers and confetti, the blood of Christ transformed, are deadly ammunition against evil. Repelled again and again, the Fariseos (including the masked Chapayekas) finally run back to the Judas figure. Here they remove their masks and place them, along with their swords and daggers, around the figure. Guided by their kin and with heads covered, they run back to the church to be rededicated to Jesus and to receive flowers. Judas, surrounded by the masks, swords, daggers, and all the refuse from weeks of ritual preparation, is ignited, and all these symbols of evil are consumed in the flames. The Pascolas, Matachinis, and the Deer Dancer celebrate the victory by dancing the rest of the day in front of the church.

On Easter Sunday during a final procession with the infant Jesus, the Fariseos make final assaults on the church. Again they are repelled and finally surrender their weapons, this time only switches and twigs. The procession continues around the plaza, and the holy figures are placed on the altar. The people form a large circle near the church cross and the head Maestro delivers a sermon from the center of the circle about the meaning of the Easter ceremony. Then the Fariseos and Caballeros go around the circle three times saying farewell until the following year.[4]

Quite in contrast to the response of the Rio Grande Pueblos to Christianity, the Yaqui Easter Festival is evidence of a complex integration of native ceremonial dance practices with Christian liturgy and beliefs. The Christian elements and beliefs may appear even to dominate, but there is evidence of the festival's continuity with important aspects of the native tradition. To more fully appreciate the Yaqui Easter Festival it must be seen in terms of its history, which stems from Sonora, Mexico, more than four centuries ago.[5]

At the time of first contact with the Spanish in 1533, the Yaquis were the northernmost of the Cahita tribes who lived along rivers in Sonora, Mexico. Their well-developed military abilities at the time of this first contact enabled them to repel a party of slave raiders under the leadership of Diego de Guzman. Yet while the Yaquis could act in concert when threatened militarily, they apparently had no general tribal organization. They lived in perhaps 80 rancherias, each consisting of about 300 or 400 persons, spread along the flood plain of the Yaqui River. Their principal mode of sustenance was cultivation, yet they maintained control of large areas of land from which they could supplement their livelihood by hunting and gathering wild foodstuffs.

Little is known of their religion at this early time, but it is believed that they sought individual visions in order to acquire personal spirits. Shamanic practices focused on curing and hunting. These shamanic performances were individually conducted affairs, while ceremonials involving the community were concerned with war, hunting, and initiation.

During the sixteenth century, there was little contact between the Yaquis and the Spanish. By 1590, Jesuit missionaries had worked their way up the west coast of Mexico as far as the Cahita tribes. The Spanish were gradually moving in this direction in conquest of lands but did not reach the Yaquis until 1608, when they suffered defeat by the Yaquis. They suffered another defeat in 1610, as the Yaquis made clear that they would not submit to Spanish power. For almost three centuries, the Yaqui people would retain something of their autonomy.

While the Yaquis did not want to be under Spanish rule, they did not reject all Spanish influence. Soon after defeating the Spanish the Yaquis asked that Jesuit missionaries be sent to them. The request was fulfilled in 1617 with the arrival of two Jesuit missionaries. The Yaquis received them enthusiastically and immediately engaged in extensive transformations of their culture as they accepted the innovations introduced by the Jesuits. Within two years, all 30,000 Yaquis had been baptized. Within 6 years, the 80 rancherias had been consolidated into 8 pueblos or towns built around the mission churches, the plan modeled on the Jesuits' idea of European towns. This town structure soon became deeply embedded in Yaqui tradition. By 1700, their mythology had incorporated the importance of the towns and the surrounding land. Each town was said to be founded by a prophet on the mandate of the gods.

The Jesuit missionaries maintained long-term commitments to the Yaqui people. They learned their language and taught the Yaqui people to read and write not only Spanish but also their own language. They made little attempt to suppress the native traditions, focusing their concerns more on the translation of prayers, the mass, and Scripture into Yaqui language. Certain Yaqui men were given positions in the church and assisted in the celebration of mass. Some also aided Jesuit attempts to force the Yaquis to attend mass.

Another important facet of the Jesuit approach was their teaching of music and introduction of dramatic presentations of Christian belief. These were New World adaptations of the widespread European miracle plays that dramatized such things as the Seven Sorrows of the Virgin Mary and the Passion of Jesus. Besides the Passion Play itself, the Yaquis performed others, such as one that told the story of the first Indian conversion in Mexico.

For more than a century, the Yaquis had a peculiar relationship with the Spanish. They had successfully defended themselves against Spanish colonial efforts and remained free of influence by civil authorities, yet they enthusiastically undertook extensive innovations under the guidance of a few Jesuit missionaries.

Not until the 1730s, when some Spaniards had established themselves as large agricultural proprietors in the land area adjacent to Yaqui territory, did the Yaqui people begin to feel the pressure of Spanish civil interests. These Spaniards were not sympathetic to the Jesuit mission program, and their anti-Jesuit disputes led to the Yaqui revolt in 1740. The great military strength of the Yaquis initially permitted them to scourge the area of Spaniards, but the Spanish strength was finally too great and the Yaquis were defeated in a battle that may have claimed as many as 5,000 Yaqui lives. The Yaqui territory then became an outpost of New Spain. For a time they continued their relationships with the Jesuits and expanded their program of innovation, which included establishment of an organized school system that extended even to advanced schooling in Mexico City of select graduates of the Jesuit school.

Finally in 1767, 150 years after their arrival, the Jesuit missionaries were expelled from the Yaqui towns. The Spanish-Yaqui differences had become too great. But in this period of a century and a half the Yaquis had undergone transformations that had completely reshaped their culture and religious traditions. They had accepted a host of techniques and forms from the Jesuits. In many cases, they invested these with their own set of meanings quite different from those taught by the Jesuits. For example, the Jesuits made extensive use of the cross. The Yaquis quickly accepted it but associated it with a female deity they called Our Mother. They treated the cross as a female deity. At the spring festival that became known as Finding the Holy Cross, they dressed it and gave it appropriate ornamentation. This identification of the cross as a mother goddess still exists.

According to Edward Spicer, a longtime student of Yaqui history and culture, the Jesuit influence in transforming the Yaqui way of life during this period amounted to an extensive enrichment of the content of Yaqui culture. The precontact concerns and worldview persisted but were enriched by acceptance of Spanish-introduced forms of expression. Three areas in Yaqui tradition underwent perceivable change during this period. There was a decrease in warfare activities; the Yaquis did not take up arms against anyone from 1620 until the Yaqui revolt in 1740. Second, because the Jesuit missions had to be supported by Yaqui labor, the considerable change in farming techniques resulted in increased production, which created a shift from subsistence farming to production of a surplus to support a modest export economy. Third, ceremonial activities were intensified as associated with the greater concentration of people in the towns and with Jesuit influence. Concentration of population was accompanied by pressures to engage in certain governmental innovations.

The great Yaqui defeat in 1740 marked the beginning of a gradual decline in Yaqui population and autonomy during a period when the Spanish government asserted increasing pressure. The Yaquis, who never simply gave up the idea of their autonomy, shifted their focus again to military activities. Population loss resulted from a number of difficulties. They were visited by epidemics of smallpox and measles, which to this time they had somehow escaped. Their military efforts frequently resulted in considerable loss of life. People began to leave the Yaqui towns to work in mines and at other jobs, assimilating into other populations in Sonora.

With the Jesuit missionaries now gone, they retained their ceremonial activities, which had been partly derived from Christian ritual forms, and continued to develop them. They were unable to maintain the high level of agricultural production achieved during the mission period. While they attempted to produce crops adequate for self-sufficiency, often even this much could not be accomplished.

Threats to the existence of the Yaquis, especially to the autonomy of the religiously sanctioned towns, engendered much effort to develop methods by which the communities could become highly integrated and protected against outside influences. Maintaining autonomy was increasingly difficult, however, and finally became impossible with the military defeat of the Yaquis in 1887. Their leader, Cajeme, was executed. This defeat resulted from, among many things, the decline in Yaqui population and the rise in strength of the Mexican government, which had been established in 1820. But development of the mechanisms for integrating and maintaining the culture continued even beyond the existence of the eight Yaqui towns. These mechanisms rested firmly on a highly developed system of religious beliefs and practices. This system, as it existed in the 1880s, was richly developed and vital to the identity of the Yaquis.

After their defeat in 1887, the Yaquis entered a period of history that saw the people widely dispersed from their homelands. Their lands were divided and distributed to Mexican settlers, and many Yaquis were forcibly deported and relocated by the Mexican government. Although guerilla activities continued for a long time after their defeat, the Yaqui communities no longer existed. The people had been dispersed in every direction. Many lost their identity as Yaquis, but others persisted. Some groups crossed the border into the United States and, by the turn of the century, Yaqui settlements had been established at three locations in Arizona. Others were located in Sonora. Not until 1906 did the Yaquis in Arizona realize that they had been granted political asylum and could reinstitute the Easter Festival and other customs that were part of

Yaqui tradition. The revival was partial but had a strong Yaqui identity nonetheless, and tradition continues in the Easter Festival still celebrated every year in the Arizona Yaqui communities.

By the 1880s, the Yaquis had enjoyed a period of a century and a half without the presence of missionaries. It was during this period that the religion of the eight towns took fullest shape. The eight towns were closely integrated and the religion may be understood in terms of four cults that took responsibility for specialized ceremonial activities. These activities were sanctioned because the accounts of their origins had become myth.

The Yaqui tradition holds that Jesus was born in the Yaqui town Belem and that he went about the Yaqui country curing and helping the people who were constantly threatened by evil beings. The principal religious order of the Yaquis was the cult of Jesus, commonly called the Lord *(El Senor)*. This cult was comprised of two societies: the Horsemen, who were devotees of Christ the child, and the Judases, devotees of the crucified Christ. This cult was responsible for the major festival of the year, the Easter Festival. Of central importance here is that the stories of Jesus were given a geographical place in the territory of the Yaquis. This served to establish the Yaqui identity and encouraged them to defend their lands against encroachments.

An indigenous religious belief of northern Mexican people had focused on a female deity associated with the rainy season of growth. With the introduction of Christianity, this belief in the figure of Mary, mother of Jesus, changed into the formation of what became, by the late nineteenth century, a cult of the Virgin. The figure on which this cult focused was called both Our Mother and Blessed Mary. She was represented both by the wooden or plaster Catholic images and by a rough cross of mesquite, which was dressed and ornamented in special devotion during the spring. This cult remained strongly associated with spring and was marked by the characteristic Yaqui use of bright colors and flowers. The most important devotees of the cult were the Matachin dancers who vowed service to the Virgin in return for help in curing. Their dance was originally introduced by the Jesuits as part of the drama that depicted the first conversion of a Mexican Indian, but this dramatic context had been lost by the late nineteenth century and was replaced by devotion to the emergent figure of the Virgin.

The cult of the dead centered on Yaqui interest by means of the ancestral dead, whom they remembered in books of family records ritually handled at fiestas. Monthly gatherings at the village cemeteries and special celebrations at the annual All Souls Feast in November integrated this cult with the other two.

The fourth cult was perhaps an aspect of the cult of the Virgin. Its patroness was the Virgin of Guadalupe, the patron saint of Mexico. This cult was primarily concerned with military activities.

The ideology and beliefs of these cults were based on or derived from the aboriginal tradition, but they were influenced, especially in form, by the Christian and European innovations introduced by the Jesuits more than two centuries earlier. In the period that ended in 1887, the Pascola and Deer Dancers were a constant presence at ceremonials throughout the year. They maintained direct continuity with the aboriginal Yaqui tradition. Their performances were unlike those of the other cults. They served in the capacity of clowns and entertainers, and maintained the lively art form of storytelling. The Pascola and Deer Dancers maintained the aesthetic and cultural vitality in the Yaqui towns through their music, dance, and stories. Notably, the Yaquis had a complex oral tradition suffused with historical and mythic events by the 1880s. The many difficult events in their history were remembered in stories that collectively comprised a narrative of Yaqui suffering and survival.

By 1887, when the Yaqui towns in Sonora fell, they enjoyed a new religious culture that had emerged from a period of development beginning at the time of the Jesuit missions more than a century and a half earlier. This religious culture arose in a historical process directed primarily by the Yaqui people themselves. They had invited and accepted broad changes, but they had generally controlled what had influenced them. The emergent religious tradition was a creative fusion of select elements from their aboriginal tradition and from the Christian-Spanish contacts they had sought. Though Christian terminology and symbols were widely used by the late nineteenth century, these seem to have been so extensively transformed by Yaqui tradition that they cannot correctly be considered Christian.

With this history as background, the Yaqui religious tradition as it appears in the celebration of Easter takes on new significance. Once reestablished as communities in Arizona, the Yaquis sought a revival of their old traditions. The cults, except for the cult of the Virgin of Guadalupe, were revived in somewhat truncated form. The major ceremonial that was revived was the Easter Festival, which was conducted by the cult of Jesus, the Fariseos. This was the revival of the primarily non-Christian tradition on the new image of the culture as it had been developed in the structure of the eight towns that created a religious history and landscape for Yaqui culture.

Yaqui communities were generally well accepted and have even been supported by the communities of Tucson and Phoenix, to which they are neighbors. The Yaquis have had to depend largely on wage labor to support themselves and thus they accepted a cash economy. They have found themselves in constant contact with non-Yaquis. In the context of these major cultural transformations, the Yaqui acceptance of actual Christian beliefs has occurred only during the period since resettlement. Still, the Yaqui church is not recognized by the Catholic church.

During Easter Week, the distinction between Yaqui and Christian beliefs takes concrete architectural form. The Yaqui and Spanish Catholic churches stand side by side in Guadalupe. During Easter Week, the plaza before the Christian church is filled with the bright lights and happy noises of a carnival, while in the plaza in front of the Yaqui church, the crucifixion and resurrection of Jesus are dramatically enacted through ritual, dance, and music. The comrades of Judas, the representatives of evil, are once again overcome by the brightly colored flowers, the transformed blood of Jesus, that are victoriously hurled at them by the people.

THE PLAINS

The horse-mounted, war-bonneted figure of the Plains tribesman has been a dominant image of the Indian in America. This romantic image has only recently begun to fade from the screens of motion-picture theaters. As a noble profile, this figure once appeared on the nickel with a buffalo on its flip side. It is this image that stands predominant in the minds of most Americans as representative of that aboriginal race of noble savages who lived in tipis on the high plains, following the endless herds of buffalo in their timeless, nomadic ways. This is the image tied to the whooping and scalping savagery directed toward innocent settlers and falling before the gunfire of the U.S. Cavalry.

While the image has some real basis in Plains cultures and American history, the archaic, timeless attributes of which we identify with are far from accurate. A broad general review of the history of the Plains tribes will serve not only to correct these impressions but also will introduce a complex past in which the religions of these people were constantly engaged in change and innovation to meet rapidly shifting needs. This noble image as well as the religions most closely identified with Plains traditions are partly products of the European presence in America.

The story begins with a general picture of the culture types that lived on the prairies and plains 1,000 years ago.[6] Evidence concerning these cultures reveals the influence of several culture types and the necessity of their adapting to ecological conditions. Along the Missouri River and its tributaries were sedentary corn-growing people. They spent most of their time near their villages tending their crops, but they also engaged in seasonal hunting. They had been influenced in both agriculture and religion by the high Mexican cultures, doubtless introduced to them by cultures bordering east of the plains region along the Mississippi River. These influences had spread northward from Mexico along the Mississippi. Among these people were the ancestors of the Mandan, who lived along the Missouri River, believed to have been the first users of the famous feathered war bonnets. Here too were the ancestors of the Pawnee, who probably originated the calumet or peacepipe. Ecological conditions were a large factor in keeping these people confined to the river corridors, along which they could grow corn and occasionally hunt to provide for their livelihood.

To the far western side of the Plains near the Rocky Mountains lived groups of nomadic buffalo hunters. Because of the ecological conditions, few of these groups existed at this early time, and they were widely scattered throughout the area. Their religious patterns were not elaborate and probably focused on individual needs in ways like vision fasting, thus emulating mythic culture heroes.

During the centuries that followed, increasing intermingling and interchange occurred among these cultures, but the most significant appearance in the Northern Plains, that is, of the people known as Sioux (Lakota or Dakota), did not occur until the seventeenth century. Before this time, these people had lived for a long time on the prairies and in the woodlands of today's Minnesota and Wisconsin. Those who lived in the western part of this area were hunters. Those in the east were hunters, fishers, and corn farmers. These are the people that we most closely associate with the war-bonneted image. Around the beginning of the seventeeth century, the Ojibwa, who lived adjacent to the Sioux, armed themselves with guns they received from white fur traders. Around 1640, they succeeded in evicting the Sioux from their area, thus forcing them to take residence in the area of the northern plains. Displaced from their homelands and way of life, these people became nomadic and lived by plundering the villages along the Missouri. In the early eighteenth century, horses, which had been introduced by the Spanish in the Southwest and Southern Plains, began to arrive in the Northern Plains in sufficient numbers to permit a major transformation of the Sioux. By integrating the horse into their nomadic way of life, they achieved a power that soon brought them into commanding control of the Northern Plains. The village cultures entered a period of decline.

The Sioux demonstrated their capacity for innovation and creative borrowing not only in terms of subsistence patterns and life ways but also in religion. The old fertility rites, which were the center of the corn-growing cultures, were transformed to fit the needs of the nomadic hunting people. Their central concern with corn was complemented by, and shifted to, a concern for buffalo and other game, while the communal orientation was complemented with a concern for the individual by giving emphasis to vision experiences. The result of these religious innovations was the Sun Dance, the most common and typical of religious practice of the Plains. The Sun Dance, performed annually, was a ceremonial effecting a world renewal that promoted prosperity for the tribe.

By the middle of the nineteenth century, the nomadic tribes of the Northern Plains, especially the Sioux, had developed a way of life that dominated the Plains. Their life way was linked with the horse and the buffalo, both of which had become dominant religious symbols. Their religious practices were focused on individual vision experiences, shamanic practices associated with hunting and curing, and the Sun Dance ceremonial, which had established itself as a tradition rooted in the era of creation. Yet, from the perspective of American history, the presence of the Sioux in the Plains and the way in which their religion had developed resulted, though indirectly, from the presence of Europeans in America. The horse, by which they had come to power, was itself a European introduction. This fact, of course, takes nothing away from the significance of the religions and cultures of the Plains people. Rather, it celebrates their capacities to engage in a history of development and radical innovation that permitted them not only to survive, but also to achieve heights of cultural and religious development.

The first half of the nineteenth century was simultaneously a period of great strength for the northern Plains cultures and of the increasing presence of American settlers. This threatening pressure was being felt by Native Americans throughout the United States. The Removal Act of 1830 resulted in displace-ment of the populations commonly known as the Five Civilized peoples (because of their great efforts to acculturate themselves to European-American ways) from the southeastern United States to the Oklahoma territory. Spo-radic military efforts by Plains tribes attempted to repel the American settlers, but such efforts eventually proved futile. As other means of resistance also began to fail, millenarian movements based on messages revealed to prophets began to erupt and spread. In the eighteenth century, a prophet arose among the Delaware and foretold that the land taken from them by the French and English would be returned to them by divine intervention. He told his people that, in the meantime, they should behave themselves, give up drinking alco-hol, and act like brothers to one another.[7]

In the early years of the nineteenth century, the Shawnee Tenskwataya, brother of Tecumseh, arose as a prophet and made similar predictions, advo-cating a reform ethic. He traveled widely and attempted to build an inter-tribal confederacy. He was killed in the War of 1812, and his efforts never developed.[8]

Numerous other prophetic movements arose and religious organizations such as the Indian Shakers of the Puget Sound area developed as a result. In the 1850s and 1860s, another movement arose around Smohalla, a Wanapum in today's state of Washington, whose alleged statements about the Indians' relationship to the earth as mother have been so often quoted. This move-ment, facing the devastation and cultural deprivation being suffered, focused on the belief in an impending destruction and renewal of the world during which the dead would return. The performance of a dance imitating the dead conjoined with millennial expectations gave rise to the Ghost Dance move-ment of 1870, widely practiced throughout the northwest United States.[9] These prophetic and millenarian movements were akin to the Ghost Dance of 1890, the best known of such movements, which was widely practiced among the Plains tribes. There is doubtless a historical connection between this and the earlier Ghost Dance movement.[10]

The origin of this movement was not in the Plains but in Nevada. Its source was a Paiute man named Wovoka, who lived on the Walker Lake Reservation. Wovoka had participated in the Ghost Dance of 1870 and he may have been familiar with Shaker religion. His background was somewhat characteristic of Native American prophets. He learned something of Paiute shamanism from his father and he practiced it among his people. He also had considerable contact with Americans. He worked for a settler family, who named him Jack Wilson, acquiring from them knowledge of Christianity. Though he traveled little outside the area of his home, he served as a bridge between cultures, typifying prophetic figures in this regard.

In the winter of 1888–89, Wovoka became ill. Coincident with a January solar eclipse that alarmed the Paiute people, he reported having had a vision in which he had gone to the spirit world and visited with the dead. He had received a millennial message and had been told what the people should do in preparation for the coming end of the world. They should perform trance dances and uphold right living by not drinking, fighting, or quarrelling. Wovoka's message spread rapidly, especially among people on the Plains, who even sent delegations to visit Wovoka in order to receive his message first hand. The Ghost Dance of 1890 brought to many cultures a message of hope in a world of increasing despair. It reflected the effects of the major transformations forced on the Plains people in the decade ending in 1890.[11]

In June of 1876 came the Battle of the Little Bighorn in which Custer suffered defeat. The Sioux still asserted the vitality of their culture. In the summer, autumn, and winter of 1876, the Plains tribes continued to defend themselves and their way of life against American troops but with decreasing success. Many Sioux surrendered in May of 1877. Bands of hostiles managed to remain free until 1881 when they too finally surrendered. The Sioux were promptly placed on reservations.

On reservations, the traditional means of attaining prestige, wealth, and rank vanished. There was no war, no hunting, and no raiding. The traditional tribal economy collapsed, and this collapse forced radical changes in diet, clothing styles, and housing. The people had no choice but to accept rations and annuities from the U.S. government, which supported them in this way while attempting to turn the people into farmers like the settlers. Because of the climate, land conditions, and temperament of the people, this effort failed miserably. The native people were forced to undergo political reorganization in order to have a means of meeting demands, and this conflicted with the traditional political organization, which itself could no longer function.

In 1883, a policy set forth by the Bureau of Indian Affairs prohibited the practice of the Sun Dance as well as other feasts and dances. Christian missionaries, especially the Episcopalians, entered to fill the gap by quickly establishing churches and schools throughout the reservations where they introduced Christianity and schooled education. The decade of the 1880s saw completion of the railroad across the plains bringing increasing numbers of settlers and visitors to the region.

The famous Buffalo Bill's Wild West Show, which also began in 1883, exploited Native Americans as curiosities for audiences throughout the United States, Canada, and Europe. Even Sitting Bull traveled with the show in 1885. The show was a major influence in spreading the Plains costume and war-bonneted images that are still familiar. It served even to teach Native Americans how they were supposed to dress and act in conformance with their growing awareness of being Indians. In the show, members of many cultures that had been enemies came together and found a common bond in their Indianness.

Another notable event of the decade was the establishment in 1887 of Indian schools such as Carlisle of Pennsylvania. Young people from many cultures were sent to these schools to be educated. The common bonds they acquired, accompanied by education in the ways of the dominant culture, prepared many of these students to lead movements for the preservation and protection of the rights of all Native Americans. The efforts of these early pan-Indian movements have actively continued to the present.

The decade of the 1880s saw the entire collapse of the traditional Sioux religion and way of life. Forced innovations had been introduced on a massive scale. The Ghost Dance came at a time of desperate need, broadly felt among the Plains people. It was quickly accepted and practiced by many as the last hope for recovery of the old ways. Throughout 1890, the people participated in the Ghost Dance in anticipation of the end of the world, a return of the dead, and a rebirth into the world as it had been of old. But this spark of hope contained, at least for the Sioux, a militant element, for it was prophesied that those who wore special ghost shirts would be impervious to the penetration of bullets. This made the U.S. government troops nervous and in this context came the senseless killing at Wounded Knee of hundreds of Sioux men, women, and children on December 29, 1890. The spark of hope carried by the Ghost Dance was snuffed out with the lives of these people.

The 1890 Ghost Dance movement, which had sought restoration of the physical, social, and cultural conditions of the past, had failed to obtain these goals, but it played a major role in bringing together and unifying people that had previously had little association. It diffused among them new religious patterns, which were adapted in a variety of ways to maintain some continuity with the old religious traditions. In the decade of the 1880s, more extensive travel by Native Americans and concentrated contact with European-American people (especially in terms of religion and education), coupled with the loss of tribal functions in warfare and hunting, promoted the rise of an Indian as distinct from a tribal identity among the Plains people.[12]

As the Plains cultures entered the twentieth century, they were forced to adjust to a complex and difficult situation. Prevented from following their old way of life, they found it impossible to simply import a new tradition. Three main paths were entered by various groups, and these paths were often combined. One path was to hold to those practices that have threads of continuity with the old tradition and to try to revive them as much as possible. Along this path the Sun Dance and other ceremonial activities were eventually revived. Another path was to encourage pan-Indian identity as much as possible and to develop traditions that were Indian in character. Numerous political organizations and ceremonial practices like the powwow arose as a result. Another path was the attempt to drop tribal and Indian identity as much as possible and to assimilate completely into majority culture. One step in this direction is the acceptance of Christianity and the acquisition of employment apart from the native reservations and communities.

One means of accommodating some aspects of all three paths was found in peyote religion, which spread across the Plains early in the twentieth century and which has continued to spread among Native Americans. As the most significant pan-Indian religion of the twentieth century it deserves further consideration.[13]

The cactus commonly known as peyote *(Lophophora williamsii)* has long been used for religious purposes by Native Americans in Mexico, where the cactus grows. Its use was introduced to the Kiowa and Comanche tribes in the southern plains about 1870. By the time of the Ghost Dance movement of 1890, it was still not widespread, but the pan-Indian awareness and broadening of friendly relationships among Native Americans throughout the Plains established conditions conducive to its diffusion. Certainly peyote religion did not spread among cultures in North America at anything near the feverish rate that had the Ghost Dance religion. During the first two decades of the twentieth century, peyote religion slowly grew among cultures throughout the Plains and surrounding areas.

An important diffusionist mechanism for peyote religion was the traveling peyote leader. A number of such figures traveled from community to community to spread their version of the religion and its ritual performances. One such leader was Quannah Parker, a Comanche chief and famous war leader. His mother, who was white, had been captured as a child and raised as a Comanche. He held out against European-American pressures until 1875. Upon his surrender, he set about establishing a new way of life for his people, a way that would combine Comanche and Anglo-American ways. He prospered as a farmer and rancher. Encouraging the pursuit of education, he sent three of his children to Carlisle. He became a friend of President Theodore Roosevelt who visited Parker and went on hunting trips with him. In 1884, Parker became seriously ill. He attributed his recovery to peyote. This made him a convert to peyote religion and he entered a lifelong effort to spread the practice of peyote religion among native people. Because Parker did not abandon his efforts to accommodate Anglo-American culture in peyote religion, peyote beliefs and practices thus incorporated some Christian elements.

Another figure instrumental in the spread of peyotism was John Wilson who was Delaware and Caddo with one-quarter French. Wilson established widespread contact among Native American cultures in the last half of the nineteenth century. He had taken up peyote religion in 1880 when, subject to a number of revelations under the influence of peyote, he was given a body of moral and religious teachings that included instructions for the ceremonial procedures and preparation of the paraphernalia. Central to such preparation was the construction of a moon-shaped altar with which his version of peyote came to be identified. Wilson was engaged in peyote religion at the time of the Ghost Dance, which he accepted as well, becoming a leader of the Ghost Dance among the Caddo. After the Ghost Dance movement had run its course, Wilson returned to his efforts to spread the peyote way until his death in 1901. Wilson's version of peyote religion also incorporated many Christian elements.

As peyote religion came to be widely established by the end of the first decade of the twentieth century, it began to draw fire from U.S. authorities. A series of legal efforts, which have yet to cease, has attempted to prevent Native Americans from practicing peyote religion. The attack has centered on the use of the peyote cactus.

Native Americans who had to fight these legal battles incorporated themselves as churches in order to gain legal status and to find shelter under the protection of religious liberty guaranteed by the U.S. Constitution. The first incorporation under the name Native American Church occurred in Oklahoma in 1918. Federal legislation introduced to prohibit the use of peyote failed to be enacted into law, but several states outlawed its use that year. More and more groups of peyotists incorporated in order to obtain a churchlike base on which to maintain the legality of their religious practices.

Peyote religion could enter any of the three paths of accommodation, even combining them in varying degrees. Most distinctive is the Indian character of peyote religion. It is not a religious practice introduced by European-American culture and its history is deeply rooted in aboriginal America. Yet it is Indian as opposed to tribal in character. This development has accommodated the growing pan-Indian awareness throughout this period in history. The most widespread feature that distinguishes peyote religion, aside from the use of peyote, is the ethic it has preached and strongly supported. This ethic focuses on problems that Native Americans recognize as threatening their existence. Notably, peyote religion prohibits the use of alcohol.

While in many cases the traditional religions could no longer be practiced, the practice of peyote religion was not difficult. It required only the acquisition of peyote and a few items of ritual paraphernalia. Furthermore, peyote religion could be construed as continuous with the old ways. The acquisition of visions under the influence of peyote was linked with the older practice of seeking visions on such occasions as puberty, preparation for war, and initiation into societies. The use of peyote has also been widely associated with medicine and thus carries on the native healing practices.

Finally, the practice of peyote religion could either exclude or incorporate Christian beliefs and practices. The peyote ritual has commonly been defended as corresponding to the Eucharist in Christianity. Jesus has been commonly identified with the spirit of peyote. Quannah Parker, for example, is reported to have said, "The white man goes into his church house and talks *about* Jesus, but the Indian goes into his tipi and talks *to* Jesus."[14]

Peyote religion is most remarkable in its capacity for meeting the complex needs of Native Americans throughout North America during this most difficult period in their history. It carries on the traditions of ritual curing and the seeking of individual visions. It has created a new ethic focused on the rejection of alcohol. It has created a new base for communal organization to support the continuity of tribal identity. It fosters the growth of Indian identity. It even provides for the embracing and nativizing of elements of Christianity. While all of these factors were fit into a matrix for rejection of the non-Indian world, peyote religion nonetheless has been capable of establishing an appearance that has permitted it to survive, although under constant threat.[15]

The threats and criticisms of peyote religion have come not only from European-American culture but also from staunchly traditional elements within tribal cultures that have seen it as too accommodating to nonnative ways.[16]

CONCLUSION

Language plays a central role in the maintenance of cultural and religious tradition. The distinction of a culture usually corresponds with language. The importance of language is evident in the examples presented. The approach of the Franciscans and Jesuits was distinguished in one way by their interest or noninterest in native languages. The Franciscans generally did not learn the Pueblo languages and their greater hostility to native religious practices is compatible with that disinterest. In such a context, it would have been difficult for the Pueblo people to have given more than compartmentalized responses to the missionaries. The Jesuits were deeply interested in learning and translating Christian materials into the Yaqui language, thus providing a context for greater assimilation of European symbols and values. European languages, particularly Spanish and English, have played important roles in providing a lingua franca for Native Americans, thus giving to people who otherwise did not easily communicate a common language. This development accompanied and helped create their sense of a shared oppression and identity as Indian. A common language has been fundamental to the development of pan-Indianism.

In these examples, there appears to be a relationship between the extent and character of intercultural contact and the reaction made by the traditions of these cultures. When cultures are threatened by oppressive forces, they apparently respond with a series of actions that serve to strengthen tradition and to intensify unity and identity. The degree and intensity of the oppressive forces is met by differing kinds of cultural responses, but at every level, religion plays a central role, for it is through religion that the worldview and broad, meaning-giving perspectives are taught, effected, and developed. The Rio Grande Pueblo people tended to retrench through their religious organizations and actions, they developed protective and isolationist mechanisms. The Yaqui extensively incorporated innovations from Spanish culture and religion, but they radically transformed these borrowings to maintain continuity with their own traditions. In the northern plains, a range of cultural influences were at play in the formulation of the Sun Dance tradition and later the Ghost Dance and peyote religions. When oppressive external pressures were reduced, acculturative processes were often accelerated.

Another important factor is the openness of a tradition to change. The Pueblo cultures appeared less open to the incorporation of change in tradition than the other examples. Perhaps this is related to their deep connection to specific lands. The Pueblos and the sedentary Plains people seem to have been less open to change and incorporation of elements borrowed from other cultures. They tended to seek isolation and protection. At the time of European contact, the Yaquis were a sedentary agriculturalist culture, but elements of a former hunting-type culture are evident in their concerns for individual visions, healing, and war. They, along with the Sioux, were the grander innovators in the examples considered.

Economic factors are significant. The difference between a subsistence and a money economy goes far beyond the simple economic aspects of alternative systems, for these systems reflect and influence the entire way of life. A subsistence economy encourages and even requires a closely unified community that may, with relative ease, avoid extensive contact with other cultures. Status, prestige, and human value are not linked to economic factors nearly as much as to knowledge, clan and society membership, and religious roles. On the other hand, a money economy encourages and even necessitates a much broader interaction among people, tending to discourage the intensive unity of small groups. Even more important, a money economy introduces a system of value, prestige, and meaning based on the possession of money and goods. The effects of such a system on religion and tradition are far-reaching.

Religious forms of expression—symbols, rituals, and stories—have histories. While these forms are commonly cast in the language of primordiality, the "in the beginning" time, they nonetheless are not survivals in the sense of being witnesses to some ancient past. Native American people may quickly reformulate their traditions including their fundamental principles and perspectives. Hence the religious symbols of the Sun Dance, the Yaqui Easter, and the Pueblo fiesta express and effect the most basic and fundamental dimensions of reality, those dimensions formulated in the beginning by sanction and action of the deities. From another view, however, these symbols, rituals, and stories arise in the history of a tradition and are constantly subject to revision and alteration. This process of change is what constitutes a living tradition.

New forms of religion emerge to meet the exigencies of history. They help in the translation of worldview and way of life. They help cultures deal with the changes, gradual or radical, that are constantly encountered. These emerging religious forms, whether protective or accommodating, are essential to bridge that seeming paradox between constancy and change, a paradox that is identified by the word tradition.

NOTES

1. Adapted from Pliney E. Goddard, *Navaho Texts,* Anthropology Papers, vol. 34 (New York: American Museum of Natural History, 1933), p. 164.

2. The principal fiesta that honors St. Joseph is annually performed on September 19. For a description and general discussion of this fiesta, see Evon Z. Vogt, "A Study of the Southwestern Fiesta System as Exemplified by the Laguna Fiesta," *American Anthropologist* 57 (1955): 820–39.

3. The historic treatment here will be based upon the account by E. P. Dozier, "Rio Grande Pueblos," in *Perspectives in American Indian Culture Change,* ed. Edward H. Spicer (Chicago: University of Chicago Press, 1961), pp. 94–186.

4. Descriptions of recent Yaqui Easter Festivals may be found in Emily Brown, *The Passion of Pascua* (Tucson: Tucson Chamber of Commerce, 1941); and Muriel T. Painter, *The Yaqui Easter Ceremony* (Tucson: Tucson Chamber of Commerce, 1950).

5. The historic treatment here will be based on the account of Edward H. Spicer, "Yaqui," in *Perspectives in American Indian Culture Change,* ed. Edward H. Spicer (Chicago: University of Chicago Press, 1961), pp. 7–93. See also Edward H. Spicer, *Pascua, A Yaqui Village in Arizona* (Chicago: University of Chicago Press, 1940); and Edward H. Spicer, *Potam, A Yaqui Village in Sonora,* American Anthropological Association Memoir no. 77 (Menasha, Wisconsin, 1954).

6. For a review of this history, see Ake Hultkrantz, *Prairie and Plains Indians* (Leiden: E. J. Brill, 1973), pp. 1–4.

7. For a review of the larger history in which this prophet arose, see A. F. C. Wallace, "New Religious Beliefs Among the Delaware Indians 1600–1900," *Southwestern Journal of Anthropology* 12 (1956): pp. 1–21.

8. See Benjamin Drake, *Life of Tecumseh and of his Brother the Prophet, with a Historical Sketch of the Shawanoe Indians* (Philadelphia: Quaker City Publishing House, 1856).

9. See Cora DuBois, "The 1870 Ghost Dance," *Anthropological Records* 3 (1939): pp. 1–151.

10. See especially James Mooney, *The Ghost Dance Religion and the Sioux Outbreak of 1890,* Smithsonian Institution, Bureau of American Ethnology, 14th Annual Report, part 2 (Washington, D.C., 1896).

11. For further discussion of the Sioux during the decade ending in 1890, see Robert M. Utley, *The Last Days of the Sioux Nation* (New Haven: Yale University Press, 1963), pp. 6–39.

12. For a study of modern pan-Indian movements, see Hazel W. Hertzberg, *The Search for an American Indian Identity* (Syracuse, N.Y.: Syracuse University Press, 1971).

13. For a comprehensive study of peyote movements, see Weston LaBarre, *The Peyote Cult* (New Haven: Yale University Publications in Anthropology, 1938; enlarged ed. New York: Schocken, 1969).

14. As quoted in Hazel W. Hertzberg, *The Search for an American Indian Identity,* p. 243.

15. For further analysis of these points, see Bryan R. Wilson, *Magic and the Millennium: A Sociological Study of Religious Movements of Protest among Tribal and Third-World Peoples* (New York: Harper and Row, 1973), pp. 414–41, 443–49.

16. For descriptions of peyote rituals, see Weston LaBarre, *The Peyote Cult* (New York: Schocken, 1969), pp. 29–56.

Epilogue

STORIES

From the viewpoint of the novel's wisdom, that fervid readiness to judge is the most detestable stupidity, the most pernicious evil.—Milan Kundera

Ethnography is autobiography.

We make up stories about others so as to better know ourselves.

Epilogue means to say in addition, a sort of postscript that suggests speech more than writing. Speech seems appropriate to stories and to Native Americans. I particularly like the ambiguity of the word story. It is commonly used to refer to myth, folktale, anecdote, history, as well as an out-and-out lie. Often we never know.

So in this saying-in-addition I use personal voice and celebrate story. This book, as are all books, is both a story about others and one facet of my personal story. I occasionally revealed my personal presence in the obviousness of first person, but the rest is, in some sense, also my story. I intend the following stories to engage each reader in his or her story.

★ ★ ★ ★ ★

One of my favorite books on Native Americans is Don Talayesva's autobiography *Sun Chief* (Yale University Press, 1942). Reading Talayesva's story has brought Hopi culture and religion to life for me and for my students. One day while I was teaching at Arizona State University I received a surprising call. I suppose it was in the mid to late 1970s. It was a woman who told me that

Don Talayesva was a guest in her Scottsdale home and he was available to come talk to my class. I was stunned that he could possibly still be alive and quickly arranged to have him come.

I met them at the campus parking lot and escorted them to my classroom. Don, sporting a red bandana tied around his steel grey hair, was feeble but walked erect. He had difficulty hearing and used this impairment to screen his interactions with others. He looked to his host, who he seemed to hear perfectly, to know if he should hear certain questions and favor them with an answer, that is, with a story. He told the stories of his life remarkably like they were written in his book, frozen versions set down 40 years before. Yet, he also awaited her cue to tell the account of his becoming Christian. His host, I've forgotten her name, told me that Don's principal activity when in her home was to read *Sun Chief.*

★   ★   ★   ★   ★

As a youth I spent many days at my grandparents' farm in southeast Kansas. My father, the youngest of seven children and many years junior to his closest siblings, remained to farm my grandparents' land. We did not live on that land however because the old ones remained there. I loved my grandparents and worked alongside both of them in the gardens and fields throughout my youth. It was the homeplace and I had roots there in the Kansas soil, roots they planted and weeded.

My grandfather, George, died at age 88 when I was in high school and my grandmother, Mattie, died at 97 when I was finishing my first graduate degree. My grandmother was such a friend to me. My dad worked several nonfarming jobs to try to keep the family with food and clothing. I was sent to the farm to work on my own. My dog Mickey was always at my side. At noon I'd go to the house where Grandma would have dinner ready for me. We'd eat and chat and enjoy one another's company. She would often tell me the stories of her youth. Every day she'd look in the local paper to read the deaths. She had a breathy way of pronouncing this word. Only rarely did she recognize the death of someone she had known, most were the deaths of their children or their childrens' children. She was baffled that she remained alive at her age.

Her death coincided with a strange undiagnosed illness my father suffered. I had come from Wichita to be with him in the hospital. It was believed he was near death. He did not know that his mother was dying. The night she died I was with him in his hospital room. He was restless, in pain, and often delirious. I stayed by the bed to comfort him, but also to keep him from pulling the IV needle from his arm and the drain tube from his stomach. Suddenly, in the middle of the night he sat up in bed and pointed to the drapes drawn over the windows. Over and over he cried out, seemingly terrified, "Mother. Mother." The next morning, more coherent, he told me he was horrified because he could see his mother at the window. Later that day we told him that she had died during the night.

After grandma died I received a bible she had kept all her years. It was wrapped in an old brown paper bag and, at the time, I glanced in it noting that there were pages of family records. I put it away only to find it again in the late 1980s shortly after I had finished writing *Mother Earth: An American Story*. I had always been interested in my genealogy, a thing I started charting when I was in high school and worked a bit more on when I was in college. It was a chart I sketched on butcher paper with notes and possible family connections traced with lines. I still have it somewhere. When the old bible surfaced I casually looked through it. Turning to the section on the births, deaths, and marriages all centering on Mattie and George, of course, I began to trace their siblings, their children, their children's children—all familiar to me, my uncles, aunts, and cousins. The following page I had never examined before. Given my interest in genealogy I can't imagine why I hadn't. This page showed who Mattie and George had descended from. My grandfather, my fathers' father, George Washington Gill, was born October 10, 1871, in Westerville, Ohio, to James Gill and Elizabeth Adams. George had five siblings: John, Hattie, Charles, Maggie, and Ettie. Mattie Delphine Fulton was born in the year 1870 in Zenia, Ohio, to Isaac B. Fulton and Ruth Ellen McGoogen. And in tiny fine script beside her name was written "born Saskwehana." My dad always told me that Elizabeth was a descendent of the presidential Adams family and that Isaac Fulton was a descendent of Robert Fulton, the inventor of the steamboat. These are his stories, now also mine, and it seems there were other stories left untold.

*　*　*　*　*

I went to visit a Navajo medicine man, a singer, who lived near Tuba City. We chatted about Navajo life and religion, about his long life and accumulated wisdom. He told me a little about his understanding of the Navajo creation. A graduate student at the time, I'd done my homework, and knew that the story he knew was not a version that had been recorded. We talked about the transmission of culture from generation to generation and he complained that he had no young Navajos learning from him. He bemoaned the fact that he was growing old and no one seemed interested in what he knew. Driven by an eagerness to contribute, a desire to help everyone more fully understand Navajos, even somehow to preserve Navajo culture for Navajos—the romantic views of a graduate student—I pleaded with this old man to allow me to record his story and to make it available through print to others.

He certainly understood what I was requesting and his answer was clear and unconditional. Stories, he said, are to be told through a living tradition. If no one is interested in them, then it is fitting they should die. But he had more to say. If lost stories should again be needed, he said, they will arise again.

I'm sure this old man is now long gone. Now I wonder about his stories.

*　*　*　*　*

When I wrote the first edition of *Native American Religions* 20 years ago what mattered most was to understand Native American people in their cultural distinctness while not becoming overwhelmed by the undeniably immense diversity. I attempted to ply the skills and insights I had learned as a scholar to the materials that somehow bore witness to these people, allowing the small but important personal experiences I had had with them to quicken my efforts, to color the stories I tell. Particularly living in Arizona, as I was at the time, I felt that cultural distinctness was important. I visited Navajo, Apache, Hopi, Zuni, Yaqui, Pima, and Papago territories and people. They didn't seem to get along with one another, or even much like one another. I listened to their languages. I read their histories. I listened to their stories. Everything I experienced told me that each of these cultures was as richly complex as any other anywhere and deserved, indeed demanded, the full measure of one's attention. To present any of these cultures, any aspect of these cultures, in some broad stroke painting of Indians or Native Americans would be to create a fiction of them all. The importance of cultural difference and distinctness remains in my view of utmost importance.

The unity or sameness bestowed even through such terms as Indian or Native American is a matter that arises from contact, is a historical issue of finding commonality in the face of common oppression or being bestowed a commonality by outsiders whose own cultural and religious survival at the time depended on constructing and projecting commonality on the others to dispel the almost overwhelming threat of rampant diversity.

Teaching Native American religions I have occasionally found myself teaching to the subjects of this study. During times when it was not acceptable to be Indian some Native Americans followed the strategy of diminishing their Indian identity and encouraging their children to be ignorant of their family and cultural heritage. By the 1980s Indian identity was becoming not only acceptable, but something to be proud of. Without knowing their native languages many of the young native people I knew were not accepted by their elders and had little access to their Indian heritage. We learned together.

During the early years of my teaching I so often heard praise heaped on Indians for their spirituality, a spirituality identified with belief in Mother Earth and Father Sky. Even the overly simplistic sound of these terms suggested to me that something wasn't quite right but I often assented to these accolades though privately puzzled by what exactly they were referring to. I knew little of such figures based on my studies and my experience in several specific cultures. Most particularly was the huge mismatch between the simplicity of these mother and father images and the daunting complexity and diversity of the specific religious traditions about which I was coming to know a little bit.

I began to collect statements related to these mother-father figures and to appraise their contexts and histories. Frankly, I found nothing contentious or even controversial here, though much of that was to follow. If one accepts that people who speak different languages, have different histories, live different lifestyles, have different religious systems, and who, in one's personal experience, constantly speak of major differences among one another are . . . let's see . . . different, then to also hold that, in some central defining way, they are somehow all the same, they all hold a deep and defining belief or practice in anything specific, demands explanation.

One explanation and certainly a valid one is that all humankind is one. This can be theologically based as in all are descended from Adam and Eve or from Changing Woman, or biologically based in that humans are a species with distinction from other species. The notion of culture as developed by modern anthropology supports and demands shared distinctive features. Cultures can be defined in many ways. Still I am unaware of any who would uphold that a culture can be comprised of hundreds of people speaking as many languages and no language in common spread over an entire continent whose common existence is not even known among them. The effort to identify culture traits to distinguish broad conglomerates of cultures is inappropriate because cultural traits do not apply in this way. Such an effort is often the confusion of cultural traits with biological ones. And this position is the grounds of racism, prejudice, and oppression. To hold that Indian religion (singular) or even Native American religions (plural) hold anything in common that is specific as to belief and practice demands a correspondence with an identifiable cultural frame. Either such beings/figures/entities as Mother Earth and Father Sky (or the Great Spirit) exist for all human beings, as argued, for example, by Jung as products of the human psyche (this is a subset of the biopsychological position), or these are beliefs of a specific culture, with their own histories and traditions. People who have languages that are not even of the same families, whose ecological bases are vastly different, whose histories are distinct and do not intersect cannot hold common cultural traits. All of modern anthropology is based on this notion. Cultural traits correspond with cultural distinctions.

Realizing this I found myself compelled to tell the story of the creation of a common cultural identity among those diverse people located in what has come to be known as North America and to focus on the role of Mother Earth in this creative construction. This was *Mother Earth: An American Story* (Chicago, 1987). That there has been such a new cultural construction in the period of contact with European-Americans cannot be contested. There was nothing like an Indian identity prior to contact and while there was communication among people of different cultures there was no effort to construct among them a common identity. Notably many of the names by which individual cultures called themselves often translates as "the people" distinguishing them from their neighbors who are not. It was only in the face of the threat of oppression and extinction that there came to be a need and a value in constructing a common identity, a common culture, a common religion among people who are at the same time culturally diverse, often even hostile to one another.

I found that Mother Earth served in this creative effort and told that story as I came to know it. It was a story that spawned others. I am sometimes a character in these stories—a trespasser, a white man, a clarifier, a culture thief.

⋆   ⋆   ⋆   ⋆   ⋆

As we age the stories of our elders pass from the world. Sometimes we learn them, often we don't. Sometimes we remember them, often we don't. As my mother aged and became the last one to have lived in the times of her stories she would laugh that the authority of her story rested on her imaginative memory and her advanced age. With a twinkle in her eye, she'd say, "Since I'm the only one left, if I say it was so, then it was so."

One Thanksgiving when I was a college student I went home for the annual feast. My aunts were always there. Really they were my great aunts, sisters to my mother's mother, Ocy Lenore Avey. I'd loved these old women my whole life. Aunt Alu, Susan Alice Avey (1877–1971), was a slight little woman who had never married. She'd stayed at home to tend to Pa, Joseph Osborn Avey, until he died. I have vague memories of him, yet my memories may be of pictures and stories about him. He was born in 1857. She lived in a tiny house on Clark Street in Cherryvale across from the park where I played and swam as a youth. I'd always drop by to chat and eat and watch her make lye soap. She had a great sense of humor and a wonderful sense of life. She was a reader for the Christian Science Church and, so far as I know, never went to a physician in her 94 years. When ill, she'd Christian Science herself into good health. My Aunt Betsy, Margaret Elizabeth Avey (1878–1971), was kind of a nutcase, always smelling of moth balls and bad breath from bad teeth, but she was pure goodness. She grew ferns and sweet potato vines. Occasionally she'd make special dishes for me like cheese-topped baked onions and raisin pie, the latter because my mother didn't like raisins. When my mother's mother died, Aunt Betsy married my mother's father, her widowed brother-in-law, and raised my mother. She was mother and aunt to my mother, a better aunt than mother according to my mother. My grandfather died when my mother was in high school. The deaths of her parents in her youth scarred my mother's life, I think, and came to obsess her with unresolved grief at the end of her life. I think she died from the pain of it.

Well, this Thanksgiving we'd eaten to the point of discomfort and somehow the conversation came around to the stories of Betsy and Alu as girls when their parents took part of the opening of the Oklahoma Strip in 1889. I'd always loved these stories. They told of the wagons lining up for the great rush and that they had somehow managed to get to the spot along the Arkansas River that would eventually be the town site of Tulsa, Oklahoma. Of course, this land passed from the family before that happened. I still have relatives who live in Tulsa. Aunt Alu, even in her nineties, was forward looking and indulged these stories only if pushed. But Aunt Betsy enjoyed telling and retelling them. I remember, on that day, them telling of their family camped out somewhere in the territory when the Dalton Brothers Gang, a notorious family of thieves, came by. Aunt Betsy got up from the table and walked about demonstrating how they held their guns pointing them at various members of the family. The Dalton Gang was finally subdued, all shot dead, while attempting a bank robbery in Coffeyville, Kansas. This town, just a few miles from where I grew up, had larger-than-life-size grainy photographs on the wall of this same bank showing the dead members of the gang laid out on the sidewalk by the bank.

My mother died a couple years ago and I received some letters that had been passed down through the family. Don't know if my mother had ever read them. She certainly never told me anything about them. Maybe they were part of the estates of Betsy or Alu. A few days after I got home from my mother's funeral I sat down to look through this little ribbon-tied bundle of letters. They were yellow and flaking. Most were letters written among the female siblings of my great grandmother, that is, my mother's grandmother. They were written in large thin cursive in both directions. This was a devise used, I think, to take advantage of what little paper was available and doubtless expensive. First write across the page in one direction then turn the page ninety degrees and write across the page over the other words. Fascinatingly, with a bit of concentration, it is quite legible.

One letter dated March 1881 was to Susan Maria Bales (b. 1853) wife of Joseph Avey, from her sister Sarah. A line from that letter reads, "Joy be to God that Ocy Lenore was born healthy and sound into the wilderness you call home. The secret of your Cherokee paramour is safe with me, though Ocy's features may one day betray you." The hint of a story swallowed by the territory and time.

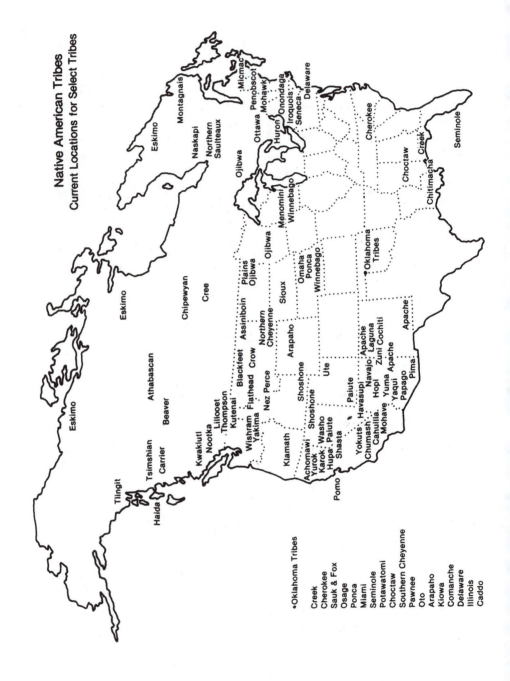

Native American Tribes
Current Locations for Select Tribes

Eskimo

Tlingit

Eskimo

Eskimo

Montagnais

Naskapi
Northern
Saulteaux

Micmac
Penobscot
Ottawa Mohawk
Huron Onondaga
Iroquois
Seneca
Delaware

Ojibwa

Chipewyan

Cree

Athabascan

Beaver

Haida

Tsimshian

Carrier

Kwakiutl
Nootka
Lillooet
Thompson
Kutenai

Blackfeet Crow

Assiniboin Plains
Ojibwa

Wishram Flathead
Yakima
Nez Perce

Northern
Cheyenne

Ojibwa

Menomini
Winnebago

Ojibwa

Sioux

Omaha
Ponca
Winnebago

Cherokee

Oklahoma
Tribes

Choctaw

Creek

Chitimacha

Seminole

Shoshone

Klamath

Achomawi
Yurok
Karok Washo
Hupa Paiute
Shasta

Pomo

Shoshone

Arapaho

Ute

Paiute

Yokuts
Chumash
Canuilla
Mohave
Yaqui

Havasupi
Hopi
Yuma

Apache
Navajo Laguna
Zuni Cochiti
Apache

Apache

Papago

Pima

•Oklahoma Tribes

Creek
Cherokee
Sauk & Fox
Osage
Ponca
Miami
Seminole
Potawatomi
Choctaw
Southern Cheyenne
Pawnee
Oto
Arapaho
Kiowa
Comanche
Delaware
Illinois
Caddo

Index